# ST FRANCIS AND ST CLARE OF ASSISI
## Passionate Lovers of Life

SISTER CLARE AGNES, osc

# St Francis and St Clare of Assisi

## Passionate Lovers of Life

ST PAULS

## ACKNOWLEDGEMENTS

Scripture quotations taken from the Jerusalem Bible, published and copyright 1966, 1967 and 1968 by Darton Longman and Todd Ltd and Doubleday & Co Inc, and used by permission of the publishers.

Excerpts from *Francis of Assisi – Early Documents, Vols 1 and 2,* edited by Regis J. Armstrong, J. Wayne Hellmann, William J. Short. Published by New City Press, London 1999, used with permission of New City Press.

Excerpts from *The Lady Clare – Early Documents*: edited by Regis J Armstrong. Published by New City Press, London, 2005, used with permission of the editor.

Translations of excerpts from the *Letters of St Clare*, 1993, copyright the author.

Illustrated by Sister Elizabeth Ruth Obbard, Solitary.

ST PAULS Publishing
187 Battersea Bridge Road, London SW11 3AS, UK
www.stpaulspublishing.com

Copyright © ST PAULS UK, 2009
ISBN 978-0-85439-750-1

Set by TuKan DTP, Stubbington, Fareham, UK
Printed by Melita Press, Malta

ST PAULS is an activity of the priests and brothers of the Society of St Paul who proclaim the Gospel through the media of social communication

# Contents

# Foreword

In a sense, this work is a process in reverse from a word becoming flesh, in that it is a lived experience now encapsulated in words. Sister Clare Agnes has travelled a meandering pathway through life and has managed to distil not just the good things that have transpired, but also the value of learning from everything that has happened thus far.

Arriving in the Community of Poor Clares in Crossbush provided her with time for prayerful reflection on this journey, along with the opportunity to enter more deeply into its significance through the Distance Learning Course she embarked upon at the Franciscan International Study Centre.

It is a story, a love story of two people who found their way to each other in friendship – Friar Francis and Sister Clare – through the love they discovered God had for them through Christ as friar.

It is the story of two ordinary people, doing ordinary things, extraordinarily well. This work illustrates what lies behind the universal appeal of Francis and Clare – arguably two of the best known saints inside and outside the Church.

What was it that virtually compelled the whole world to go after them? Francis was no miracle worker, no orator, not a revolutionary – and Clare spent her life in the contemplative solitude of San Damiano, seemingly cut off from what was happening outside.

As this work shows, when that question is faced the answer is patently simple, though like all truly simple ways, never easy! For whatever reason devotees of things Franciscan soon discover that all that they admire in Francis and Clare prompts them to say – I could do that! What Francis and Clare both exemplify is that the actual doing of what they did was preceded by something crucially important. They had to have the heart for it. It is not enough to feel that this is what I want, it has to be heart-felt. Both of them were able to declare unequivocally – This is what I long for with all my heart!

Prior to his conversion Francis wanted not just everything but the best of everything – after his conversion he wanted everything and the best of everything, so what had changed? Grace had shown him who everything was, not what! Intimacy with Abba through Christ as friar. It was Francis' whole-hearted embracing of this, lived out in the streets of Assisi, that sparked the attention of Clare, who later would counsel us – Give yourselves totally to him who gives himself to you totally! There is no way the Franciscan vision of Gospel life can be experienced as liberating and as brim-full to overflowing if we haven't the heart for it!

For both of them this gift of a heart broken open into fullness was their awareness of the crucial role the Holy Spirit would play in their lives. Aware that through the Eternal Word, God knows totally who God is and by the Spirit of them both, God enjoys being God – Francis and Clare discovered mind and heart renewed to the fullness of God as Abba, through Christ as friar, in the Spirit who persuades them that they too are beloved of Abba. We can all do this, if we have the heart for it!

*Austin McCormack,* OFM
*Feast of St Francis 2008, Chilworth*

# Introduction

This book is about two people who have really inspired me, and whom I have grown to love. I firmly believe that it is very helpful to our human growth to have a role model. It is surely good to meet particular people who can fill you with enthusiasm, lead, and guide you on a path that leads to happiness and goodness and truth. Such people need to be truly human in their life style and wholly secure in themselves and with others. Such models are St Francis and St Clare. These two had a deep love for God and a deep love for each other. Not the sort of love that is possessive or erotic, but they were united because they both looked at Jesus Christ. He was constantly before the eyes of their minds. He was their role model and true love, and that's why we can see a way to fulfilment through watching how they did it. This is despite the fact that they lived 800 years ago between the twelfth and thirteenth centuries.

That period in history is sometimes called the Dark Ages. The Church was dominated by a great greed for wealth. The Papacy was involved in continual political struggles with the Emperor over possession of land. Priests' lives left much to be desired, morally speaking. They were ill-educated and as a result the people were left to find salvation as best they could. Groups sprang up to try to counteract these tendencies, professing to return to the ways of the early Christian Church, but they overdid things and became heretics.

The old feudal system had largely disappeared, and many of the country people flocked into the towns and cities looking for work and wealth. This led to great poverty among them, as there was not enough work to go round either in the country or the towns. In addition to this, the population was increasing all the time. It was during these years that the merchant class grew in numbers and in wealth. The nobles were still the aristocrats, but the merchants held the money.

This was the era of the Crusades by which the Church appealed for men to go and rescue the Holy Land from the clutches of the Moslems who had captured the city of Jerusalem, sacred to them as well as to Christians. Thousands of men were involved, and very many lost their lives in the violence that ensued.

It seemed that society was rudderless. People had somehow lost the meaning of life, and their main struggle was to keep themselves alive, with the poor scratching for food and the rich safeguarding their money and searching for ways to make more. Certainly the Christian message of the Gospel was neither widely known nor lived.

Into this mayhem there arose these two great lights – Francis and Clare, who from very small and insignificant beginnings, brought meaning and direction back into their society.

The parallels between the Middle Ages and the twenty-first century are pretty obvious. One has only to read the papers or watch television to see the same greed, materialism, an increase of poor people and violence.

It is my conviction therefore, that Francis and

Clare are very relevant to our world today. Their message was of peace – the peace of God which passes all understanding. They offered something much more lasting than the everlasting pursuit of what pleases 'me' – namely, a relationship with God, with other people and with the whole of creation that is more satisfying than anything or anyone else.

The purpose of this book, therefore, is to familiarize people with these two people and with their attitude to life, their faith and their love. I have this vision of other Francises and other Clares springing up to rejuvenate our society and restore it to true happiness. My hope is that one or two will be stimulated by what they read of the stories here to set out on the Way of Christ that Francis and Clare trod. Life, which these two were so passionate about, was an integral whole. God, his Son Jesus, the Holy Spirit, men, women, the earth and its beauty, friendship and all human love had a place in their minds and hearts. At the centre was Christ, who said *I am the Way, the Truth, and the Life.* To rediscover this is to be truly happy, and like them to love all life passionately.

*Sister Clare Agnes, OSC*
*4 October 2008, Feast of St Francis*

# Ambition for Life
# The story of St Francis

"I have come,
so that they may have life
and have it to the full."

*John 10:10b*

## CONVERSION

### Assisi

Assisi is a small town almost in the centre of Italy, built on the edge of Mount Subasio which overlooks the green Spoleto valley through which the upper reaches of the River Tiber run. The stone houses today with their warm convex tiles, are very much thrown together in the haphazard way that they were in the twelfth and thirteenth centuries. The narrow cobbled streets are steep and frequently break into long flights of steps. It has the air of a medieval town, in spite of the many cars that negotiate an intricate one-way system.

### Medieval Political and Religious climate

Modern Assisi may resemble its medieval image, but in the twelfth and thirteenth centuries the political and religious atmosphere was very different. All Christians in Italy were Catholics. The 'enemies' were the Moslems, who tried to enlarge their influence in Europe. The Pope was not only the most powerful religious leader, but also a formidable political one as well. He was very wealthy and owned much land in Italy. He was frequently opposed by the Emperor of the Holy Roman Empire, who also had land in much of Italy. Assisi had been governed by the Emperor's representative, Conrad von Urslingen, who had been excommunicated for opposing the pope. When he eventually submitted to Pope Celestine III, the whole of Assisi's allegiance was transferred to the pope. The merchant class were now free from the rule of the Emperor. They set about violently attacking the property of the nobility, who had to flee from the violence to Perugia, a town twenty-five kilometres away, which was a Papal state.

Times were indeed dark and troubled on both the political scene and in the Church. If they had newspapers like ours in those days, you would have read headlines like these:

**POPE CALLS ON ALL CHRISTIANS TO TAKE UP ARMS AGAINST MOSLEMS IN THE HOLY LAND.**

**SCANDAL OVER CLERGY MORALS**

**HERETICS EXCOMMUNICATED**

**RISE OF GROUPS WHO LIVE IN POVERTY MOSTLY HERETICS**

**EMPEROR AND POPE AT LOGGERHEADS OVER LAND OWNERSHIP**

**PEOPLE FLOCK TO NEW TOWNS TO FIND FOOD AND WORK**

**BARTER IS OUT – MONEY IS IN!**

**ANGER AGAINST BISHOPS FOR TAXING FARM LAND**

**MERCHANTS RISE UP AGAINST THE ARISTOCRACY**

The Church was the most influential body, but it betrayed the teaching and way of life of Christ. It was rich and powerful. Yet it paid little heed to the poor.

Its senior clergy sought power and the lower ranks were ill educated and immoral. The vices of human nature which are common in our day – violence, materialism and the misuse of sex were found in this religious society and beyond. Anticlericalism was everywhere, and new religious groups of lay people sprang up in protest at the betrayal of the Christian message. All these movements began as attempts to bring the Church back to its Apostolic roots, but many ended in being, as it were, too much of a good thing, going their own way, heedless of any warnings. So they were excommunicated as heretics. It is important to reckon with these waves of protest against the problems of the Church in order to appreciate what St Francis eventually did.

### Pietro Bernadone – Francis' father

In this climate during the latter part of the twelfth century, Pietro Bernadone set up his business as a merchant of expensive cloths. He sold these at great profit to the clothes-loving rich of Assisi. He went regularly to France to be sure of getting the best materials. We might call Pietro one of the 'nouveau riche'. He was not an aristocrat, nor was he a peasant. He belonged to a new social class of merchants. It was they who were, in fact, the richest in terms of the new way of acquiring goods with money, instead of by bartering. It was in 1182, while Pietro was away in France, that Pica's baby was born. She had him baptised Giovanni, (John) but when his father returned he nicknamed him Francesco (Francis), and the name stuck.

## Francis' youth

Francis received only about two year's formal education. He was taught, with other boys, by the priests of the church of San Georgio. He learnt to read and write and memorize in Latin, through the psalms and other passages of scripture. When he was thirteen his father initiated him into the cloth business, and he used to travel with him to the great fairs in France and elsewhere, buying cloth. From these journeys he became fluent in French, a language he loved to speak and to sing.

Back in Assisi he soon became the leader of the gang of young people. They would carouse in the evenings, their songs echoing off the walls of the houses. His friends enjoyed his good humour and witty speech, his exotic clothes, his love of singing the love songs of the Troubadours. They would feast in grand style, thanks to the money Francis had in his pocket, and drink and revel until the early hours. Naturally his parents worried. Would he ever settle down and seriously prepare to take on the cloth business with his father?

## Francis' ambitions

By the age of twenty Francis already had quite a good business head, and would serve in the shop quite often. In spite of his reckless ways with his friends, he had great sympathy for the poor, and would often help them. But Francis did not intend to become a merchant. He set his sights on better and more exciting things. He wanted above all to be a knight by getting himself honoured in battle. If he succeeded it would mean a step up the social ladder, as well as fame and riches. The opportunity soon came when Perugia rose against Assisi in 1202. There was a big battle in Colestrada, the territory between the two towns. Francis was unfortunately captured in this battle, and chained with many fellow prisoners. These men were utterly depressed by their situation, but Francis made fun of it all. They were put into a damp cell and remained there for one year. One of his fellow prisoners was very aggressive, and the others decided to avoid him. Francis, however, befriended him and not only cheered him up, but managed get the others to accept him again.

Eventually a truce was made and his father paid a ransom to free him, but by this time Francis was very sick, probably with malaria. For about a year his mother looked after him. His zest for life had gone. He had had time to reflect, and his thoughts depressed him. He had nothing to aim for, no ambition any more. He no longer took pleasure in the beauties of nature as he had done before or even in the company of his friends. He thought of himself as worthless, and was not entirely happy with the way of life that he had lead before.

## The dreams

At that time – in 1205, when Francis was twenty-four, there was a certain Count Walter de Brienne, who was about to set out on a project which involved fighting for the Pope's interests against the Emperor's. Francis was once more fired with the ambition to be a knight and become immersed in the world of chivalry and glory. He bought the most expensive and splendid suit of armour, and a fine horse and rode off to Apulia to find Walter. On his way there he had a powerful dream. He was in a palace which was filled with splendid knightly armour, with shields and spears glittering from the walls. When he asked who all this belonged to, he was told that all of it, including the palace, belonged to him and his knights. Francis was delighted and took is as a good omen for his future. "I know I will become a great prince," he said.

So he arrived at Spoleto, twenty-two miles south of Assisi. That night he fell ill again – maybe a recurrence of malaria. He had another dream. This time he definitely heard the Lord say to him: "Francis, who can do more for you, a lord or a servant, a rich person or one who is poor?" Francis gave the obvious answer and received another question: "Why then, are you abandoning the Lord for a servant and the rich God for a poor mortal?" This threw him, but prompted him to ask: "Lord, what do you want me to do?" It was the first definite realization that his life was destined to take a radical about-turn, but he did not yet know how. He was told to return to Assisi, where he came to understand that his dream would have a spiritual outcome which God would carry out in him.

**Francis' heart is stirred by the Lord**

However, he found none of this uplifting. Back in Assisi he fell once more into a depression and wandered about listlessly. He was confused and aimless. The young men of the town had not forgotten how he used to lead them in revelry and pay for their good food and wine, so he was drawn back by them into the old ways and made King of the Banquets. For a while that summer he played the part, but his

18

heart was not in it. One evening, after a huge meal which Francis had arranged, they walked through the street, singing, as was their wont. Francis, however, lagged behind, preoccupied with his own thoughts. Suddenly he was touched by the Lord with so much tenderness that he was unable to speak or move. He stood stock still. He was completely held in this gentle touch of God. His friends laughed at him and teased him about being in love. Francis told them that he was indeed in love, but not with a future wife. His love was his Lord, to whom he felt drawn with every fibre of his being. The tenderness that he had experienced followed him everywhere and he was drawn by it to find some quiet and secret place in which to pray. His way of living changed too. He became even more generous than before in giving alms to the poor. He would give money or part of his clothing. Once, when his father was away, he heaped the table with bread to give away to the hungry. The focus of his ambition was changing.

About this time, on a pilgrimage to St Peter's in Rome, seeing the poor people crowding the steps, begging, he swapped his rich clothes with the rags of a poor man, and sat with the others, eating with them and begging as they did. He was very peaceful as he rehearsed the poverty that he would soon be inspired to adopt. However, his friends were horrified and eventually managed to dissuade him from this embarrassing escapade. When he regained his own clothes he watched others throw in a few coins at the high altar, but he threw in a whole handful of money because he thought God should be honoured in a special way. For the same reason he would give liturgical vestments to priests, especially to those who were poor. The growing intensity of his love for Christ drove him to these eccentricities, and would do so all his life. So he prayed to know God's will for his future.

He received a strange answer to his prayer. The Lord was inspiring him to turn away from the things he had always liked and lived for: fashionable expensive clothes, a good time with friends, plenty of food and drink, ambition to better himself. Only when he had relinquished these things would he be able to understand what God's will was for him.

## The Leper

The thing that most revolted him was the sight and smell of lepers. Normally he would avoid such people by putting two miles between himself and them. Though he would give them money through another person, he could not look at them, and would hold his nose against the stench. Soon after his realization that God had some special plan for him a surprising thing happened. This was to revolutionize his life completely. He was riding along outside Assisi and came face to face with a leper. This time, however, he made himself dismount. He not only gave the man a coin, but also kissed his hand as he did so. Furthermore he allowed the leper to give him a kiss of peace. A few days later he visited the lepers' hospice. He gave them a lot of money, kissed their hands, and from then on would serve and befriend them. What had been bitter now seemed sweet. He always regarded this particular event as a major turning point in his full conversion to God. He never forgot it, and at the end of his life he wrote in his *Testament:*

When I was in sin, it seemed too bitter for me to see lepers. And the Lord himself led me among them. And when I left them, what had seemed bitter to me was turned into sweetness of soul and body. And afterwards I delayed a little and left the world.

First, this action led him to want to pray. He found a cave outside the town where he could pray to his Father in secret. But it was not all sweetness. He was very much tempted to return to his former life and sins. He tossed and turned in his mind whether he would be able to continue on the path God seemed to be leading him.

## The San Damiano Crucifix

One day he was walking along about a mile below Assisi when he came across a tiny church, known locally as San Damiano. He went in and saw suspended from the roof a very large painted cross – more like an icon. Light shone from the figure of Christ. His eyes were open and seemed to look straight at Francis. It was a crucified AND glorious Christ. Standing underneath his arms were figures of Our Lady, St John, Mary Magdalene and Mary of Cleophas and the centurion. They were all smiling! But Francis only saw the Christ figure and he began to pray intensely, thus:

Most High, Glorious God,
enlighten the darkness of my heart,
and give me Lord, a correct faith a certain hope,
a perfect love, sense and knowledge
so that I may carry out your holy and true command.

As he prayed, he heard the figure of Christ address him: "Francis, don't you see that my house is falling into ruin? Go, then, and rebuild it for me." Amazed and trembling, he replied: "I will do so gladly, Lord." He thought it meant that it was this particular church that needed rebuilding – which indeed it did. Only much later did he realize the wider significance of the instruction, and that it applied to the People of God. This was a very personal meeting between Christ and Francis which filled him with great joy. The icon itself had made a lasting impression on him, and ever after, to the end of his life, his heart was deeply moved when he remembered the Lord's Passion.

### Francis and his father

Now he had a job to do – rebuild this church of San Damiano. First, he needed money to buy stones. So he returned to his father's shop, selected cloth of different colours, got on his horse and rode seventeen kilometres to Foligno. There he sold the cloth and the horse, and on his return he gave the money to the priest at San Damiano. However, the priest feared the reaction of Francis' father for he didn't trust this sudden conversion. He refused to take the money, so Francis just threw it on the windowsill. Then he begged the priest to let him stay there with him. Reluctantly the priest agreed.

Not without reason did the priest fear Pietro Bernadone. When he realized that his son had taken and sold the cloth and the horse and was living at the church, he came after him. Francis had foreseen this, so he hid in a cave for a month, and prayed. He only ate when a friend brought him some food. The Lord filled him with great happiness though he still did not know what he was to do. One day he left the cave and went back into the town. His former friends laughed at his bedraggled appearance; young lads threw stones and mud at him, thinking he was mad. His father heard about all this and when he found him, he dragged him home and locked him up in chains in a dark place for days. Eventually Pietro had to go away on business and his mother released Francis, who went straight back to San Damiano. On his return, the father took proceedings again him for the loss of the money, but Francis refused to appear before the magistrates. In any case, they said: "Because he is in the service of God we no longer have any jurisdiction over him." So Pietro complained to the Bishop who summoned Francis to give an account of himself. Francis agreed, "I will appear before the lord bishop, because he is the father and lord of souls."

## The Bishop

So Francis went to see the Bishop straight away. The Bishop was very pleased to meet him and gave him sensible advice: "If you truly want to serve God you must return the money to your father. That is all he wants. Just have courage and trust in the Lord for he will give you whatever is necessary for what he wants you to do in the Church."

Francis fetched the money from the windowsill where he had thrown it and gave it to the Bishop with his father and a crowd of people looking on. "My Lord," said Francis to the Bishop, "I will gladly give back to my father all the money acquired from selling his things, and even all my clothes." With that, he stripped off all his clothes and standing there naked before the Bishop and his father and the crowd he said: "Until now I have called Pietro Bernadone my father. But now I propose to serve God and say *Our Father who art in heaven* not my father, Pietro di Bernardone."

Pietro was cut to the quick by these words. As he took himself off home, carrying the clothes, the people shouted after him for leaving Francis standing there naked. But he was unmoved, so angry was he. From this time on there is no further mention of either Francis' father or mother, and no account of reconciliation. Francis is on his own with his God.

The bishop, however, impressed by Francis' determination, realized that he was inspired by God to act in this way. He covered him with his own cloak, and promised to help him in whatever he discerned was God's will for him to do.

Francis was now free and full of joy. He made himself a hermit's habit and continued fixing the church of San Damiano. This time he went around the town begging for stones. Not only that, he took a bowl and also begged for his food. What he received in the way of scraps revolted him, but he overcame himself, and when he started to eat, the mess in the bowl seemed delicious. The bitter had become sweet again. He thought of Christ who was born poor, lived very poorly and was naked and poor on the cross, and this encouraged him. His one aim was to live like his Crucified Lord had lived, for he realized that he had been gifted by God to want to do this. It was love in return for love.

### An important premonition

So he merrily continued rebuilding the church of San Damiano. One day when he was high up on the walls, he saw a group of peasants passing, and he called out to them in French: "Come and help me build this church, which in the future will be a monastery of ladies through whose fame and life our heavenly Father will be glorified throughout the church." This happened very soon after his conversion. He must have told this story to Clare, because in her *Testament* she speaks of this prophesy being fulfilled as San Damiano became filled with Sisters. It was something that she obviously treasured, because it was a confirmation of God's will for her.

## CO-OPERATION

### Francis is touched by the Gospel of poverty

So, was Francis to spend his time just mending tumbledown churches? He did not know, so he went on doing it. One of the churches he repaired was outside the city of Assisi, in a wooded part of the countryside. The place was called the "Portiuncula", which means 'Little Portion'. On this piece of land was a small chapel, dedicated to Our Lady of the Angels. It was deserted at that time, so Francis, because he had a great devotion to Our Lady, began to stay there continually. One day, while he was at a Mass being said in that chapel, he heard the Gospel where Christ instructs his disciples what to do when they went out to preach. This is what he heard:

> *Provide yourselves with no gold or silver, not even with a few coppers for your purses, with no haversack for your journey or spare tunic or footwear or a staff.* Matthew 10:9-10

When the Mass was over he asked the priest to explain the Gospel to him, which he did, line by line. This message from God through the Gospel filled him with energy and life, and made him very happy indeed. "This is what I want! This is what I seek; this is what I desire with all my heart!", he cried out. There was nothing half-hearted about Francis. He took this message literally and changed his hermit's garb for a single tunic, and discarded his sandals and walking stick. His leather belt went flying, and in its place was a piece of old rope round his waist. Thus clothed, the rich poor man went off to preach this new life he had discovered. As he went among the people his greeting was: "May the Lord give you peace." This was his message as he urged them to turn back to God, who is full of compassion, mercy, peace and love. He was filled with the Holy Spirit and able to touch the hearts of many as he helped them to understand Gospel values.

**God sends Brothers to Francis**

Two years after he had surrendered himself to the service of God, some men of Assisi were moved by his message and wanted to lead the same sort of life. The first was Bernard, a rich man of some importance in Assisi. He had known Francis in his heyday and was impressed by the change that had taken place. So he decided to invite him to stay at his house. He had a bed put in the room where he slept, and when they both retired, they both pretended to be asleep. When Francis was sure Bernard was asleep, judging by the snoring, he got up, knelt on the floor, and prayed thus: "My God and my all!" He repeated the same prayer all night long. In the morning Bernard was convinced that Francis was genuine. He said: "This man truly is from God." Immediately he got his things together, sold them, and with Francis' help, gave away all the money to the poor.

While they were doing this, much to the delight of the poor people who thronged round this bonanza, a priest called Sylvester, who had previously sold Francis some stones for the rebuilding of San Damiano, came up grumbling. He complained that Francis hadn't given him enough for the stones, so Bernard took great handfuls of the coins and gave them to Sylvester. Then he did it a second time, saying: "Is that enough now, Lord Priest?" And Sylvester replied that indeed it was, and went home chortling over his good fortune.

Some days later, however, Sylvester had second thoughts. He considered that old man that he was, he still wanted to be rich and fill his life with material things. He saw that Francis was free from all that, and had joyfully given it all up because God was the centre of his life. Inspired by Francis, Sylvester wanted to change his life radically; so at first he did penance at home and eventually joined Francis' band of Brothers.

Meanwhile, Francis and Bernard went to the church of St Nicholas to try to find out from the Gospel what they should do. Another man called Peter joined them. They prayed and then opened the Gospel three times. This first opening said this:

> *If you wish to be perfect, go, sell everything you possess and give to the poor, and you will have a treasure in heaven.* Mark 10:21

This confirmed Francis in the way he had begun, and he was delighted. The second opening also enjoined poverty:

> *Take nothing for your journey, neither staff nor haversack nor bread nor money.* Luke 9:3

The third opening revealed Francis' desire to follow Christ to the Cross:

> *If anyone wants to be a follower of mine let him renounce himself and take up his cross and follow me.* Matthew 16:24

As they left the church, confident in the Lord and excited, Francis exclaimed: "Brothers, this is our life and rule! Let's go and get on with it!"

## The joy and vigour of the Brothers

Soon there were twelve Brothers and the light of the Franciscan life began to grow. It was to be the impetus needed to repair the Church. What was so attractive about Francis and the first few Brothers? It was above all their joy. They had freely chosen to live those three Gospel texts. They wanted above all the *treasure in heaven*. The sure way to bring it about on earth was to be free from the desire for any kind of possessions. Poverty made room for God to take over their lives. They wanted to rely on God to give them what they needed to live and not go around with provisions for the future in a rucksack. They wanted above all to be like Christ in his suffering and rejection, because he was their Brother. They would go with him to the end. So they had a deep inner peace, even when they were laughed at and ridiculed. Francis encouraged them in other Gospel values, so they liked to be together in a community. It was a pleasure for them to be able to care for each other. They had a genuine love for one another and for all who came to them. They were able to forgive when wronged and be patient when the going was hard. Seeing Francis take such a delight in prayer, they wanted to imitate him. Thus they became men of deep spirituality. Caught from Francis, they had a kind of fiery energy that was very attractive. It filled them with a joy that was the magnet which drew others.

## They seek approval of the Pope

Unlike many of the other groups of men and women who began by professing poverty, but who later went against the teachings of the Church, Francis realized that he needed to get Pope Innocent III to approve what they were doing and give them permission to preach. In 1209 they walked to Rome, a journey that took them six weeks. Francis was twenty-seven. The Bishop of Assisi introduced them to an influential Cardinal, who liked Francis immediately. It was he who arranged for him and his Brothers to see the Pope. The Church at that time was in great need of renewal, and the Pope at this time was very concerned to find means to revive the Gospel message among the people. A few days before he met Francis, he had a vision of a religious man, small and scorned, who was propping up the Lateran basilica which was about to collapse. When he met Francis and saw this small band of rather scruffy, poor men, totally dedicated to Christ and his Gospel, he realized that these men, under the leadership of Francis, could be instrumental in bringing about the renewal that was so badly needed. So he quickly granted their Gospel Form of Life, but not without fears that the high standard they were setting themselves would be too hard for them. This approval gave them great confidence.

> Immediately visiting towns and villages, Francis began, with the authority now granted him, to preach passionately and to scatter the seeds of virtue.                           2 Celano XI:17

### Rivo Torto

Back in Assisi they went to live at Rivo Torto, a small hut about five miles from the town. It was so small that Francis had to mark each Brother's place with chalk, so that there would be room for all of them to sleep and pray peacefully. From there they went out each day working to earn their food for Francis would not allow them to accept wages in money. They preached the Good News of the Gospel in and around Assisi. When they returned in the evening they would eat a frugal meal from what they had been able to beg, and then spend the evening in contemplative prayer.

Francis became a very popular preacher because he did not harangue people. He first made sure of the truth of what he said by doing it himself. Then he could convince others in a forthright way. The result was that not only did the poor listen to him, but even educated people were amazed at his power of speaking of Truth, and they regarded him as a 'person of another age'.

One day, while the Brothers were immersed in silent prayer, a man with a donkey barged into the

Rivo Torto. He urged the donkey inside, shouting: "Get in there – we will do well in this place!" Francis was very annoyed at this disturbance because he realized that if they did not have space for prayer and quiet, they could not do the work God had called them to do. So they moved down the road, about two or three miles, to the Chapel of St Mary of the Angels, known as the Portiuncula, or Little Portion. It belonged to some Benedictine monks nearby, who wanted to give it to Francis. But Francis did not want to own anything, so he rented it from the Benedictines for a basket of fish and some oil each year. It was now 1210, and from then on Francis and his Brothers made their home there. In the surrounding woods they built little huts where they slept and prayed. It became the place in all the world that Francis loved best. It was at this time that Francis called them Friars Minor to indicate their low estate in society and to identify them with the poor.

## Meeting with Clare

In the year 1210, at the beginning of Francis' new life, a momentous meeting took place. Francis would go into Assisi to preach in the Cathedral of San Rufino. Nearby lived the daughter of an aristocratic family, Clare di Offreduccio. She was sixteen years old, eleven years younger than Francis. She would go to the Cathedral and hear him make the Gospel so vivid and true that she sought him out to learn more. Over two years they met, each with a friend as chaperone. Clare, 'who relied on his sacred admonitions and received whatever he said of the good Jesus with a warm heart,' soon wanted to live the same kind of life as Francis. Eventually she did this in the only way possible for a woman in those days, but the story of how he enabled her to become a contemplative and foundress of a new Order for women is in another chapter.

## The Brothers go out on Mission

When the group was still small Francis called them to him and divided them into pairs. He spoke to them about his ideals of spreading the kingdom of God, and how they must keep clear of the values of the world to follow Christ more closely. Then he said: "Go, my dear brothers, two by two, into different parts of the world. Give the people the greeting of peace, and invite them to change their lives and turn to the God who loves them."

He encouraged them to be patient in trials and very confident that the Lord would not let them down. Willingly the Brothers accepted this 'obedience', and Francis hugged each one and recited this verse of Psalm 55: *Cast your care upon the Lord, and he will sustain you.*

After a short time Francis wanted to see them again, so he prayed that they would soon return. His prayer was answered, and they all came together at the same time. They were rejoicing and giving thanks to God for all the good things that the Lord had done through them.

Over the years that followed hundreds of men flocked to join this new movement. At first they limited their work to Italy, but when in 1217 Francis summoned them all to the Portiuncula for a Chapter Meeting, they decided that they would go further afield. Men were sent to Germany, France, Hungary and Spain. Some went to Morocco to preach to the

Moslems, but they were not welcome and became the first Franciscan martyrs. Francis himself had wanted to go on that journey, but he got sick and had to turn back. On hearing of the cruel death of these men he exclaimed: "At last I have five true Friars Minor!"

## Francis visits the Sultan at Damietta

Six years after his conversion Francis had wanted to go and preach to the Moslems and tell them the Good News. He was ambitious to become a martyr, like those first five Brothers in Morocco. He set off by ship, but never arrived because the ship was wrecked in the high seas of the Adriatic. Seven years later, however, Pope Innocent III was really keen to drive the Moslems out of the Holy Land, and especially out of the Holy Places in Jerusalem. So he asked all the faithful European Christians to fight the Moslems and free Jerusalem, and make it safe for Christianity to flourish in the Holy Land. History calls this war the Fifth Crusade.

Francis took this call of the Pope as his opportunity to talk to the Moslems about Jesus. He went to Damietta in North Africa not as a crusader-knight but as a missionary. It was a terrifying place for Christians to be in. The Sultan, Malek al-Kamil, had promised his men a gold coin for every Christian head they brought to him!

Taking Brother Illuminato with him, they boldly walked across the enemy lines to speak to the Sultan about the Gospel. The Moslem soldiers of course, took them prisoner on the way there, but Francis said to them: 'I am a Christian, take me to your master'. They first beat them with whips and put them in chains. Then they dragged them to the Sultan. He asked them who they were and why they had come. Francis did not beat about the bush, but told him straight that no man had sent him, but the Most High God, to show them the way to salvation. Then, fearlessly, he preached to him with great firmness about the Trinity and about Jesus

The Sultan was impressed and listened, but though he accepted Francis, he could not take to his message about Christ for political and religious reasons. Francis glimpsed a moment of hesitation in the Sultan, so he asked him to have a huge fire prepared. Then he said, he and one of the Sultan's priests would go into it, so that it would become clear which faith were the more certain. The Sultan, naturally, would not agree to this, especially as he had seen one of his priests quietly disappear! So Francis proposed to go into the fire alone, and added: "If I come out of the fire unharmed, you and your people will come over and acknowledge the power of Christ. If I burn, then it will be because of my sins." The Sultan again refused, because he feared that his people would rebel against him. Nevertheless, because he admired and respected Francis, he offered him many precious gifts for the Christian poor. Francis, spurning worldly possessions, and unaccustomed to being loaded with the responsibility of money, refused. So Francis and Illuminato continued their journey to the Holy Land where they experienced the very places where Jesus had lived and died.

## Arguments about poverty – Francis resigns as leader

When he returned to Assisi he discovered a great change among the men he had left. Priests and educated men had joined the Order. They were not able to accept the strict life of poverty that was Francis' dream. They needed permanent buildings in which to study and books and parchment to prepare for their work of preaching. So in 1220, Francis called another Chapter of all the 5,000 Brothers who had joined him. It was called the *Chapter of Mats*. Francis deliberately made no provision for this huge meeting, so huts of wattle and daub were hastily put up. The local towns and villages generously supplied them with food. The Lord Cardinal Hugolino, who later became Pope Gregory IX, was there too. The newly educated Brother Priests tried to persuade Francis to adopt one of the old well-tried Rules, such as that of St Benedict or St Augustine, which taught a proper way of living. Francis was deeply hurt and not a little angry. He stood up and spoke to the whole assembly thus:

My Brothers! My Brothers!
God has called me by the way of simplicity and showed me the way of simplicity. I do not want you to mention to me any Rule, whether of St Augustine or of St Bernard or of St Benedict! And the Lord told me what he wanted. He wanted me to be a new fool in the world. God did not wish to lead us by any way other than this knowledge, but God will confound you by your knowledge and wisdom. But I trust in the Lord that he will punish you, and you will return to your state, to your blame, like it or not.

Assisi Compilation, 18

The Cardinal was shocked to hear this, and the Brothers became afraid. The great argument about poverty had begun, and goes on to this day. It caused Francis to resign leadership of the Brothers, and to want to live under a Superior, in obedience. He felt they had rejected him, and the hurt stayed with him as long as he lived. He was now sharing in the rejection that Christ experienced, and this was his consolation.

## Francis writes two Rules

Nevertheless he took a keen interest in the development of things. During the following year he wrote a Rule which was filled with the inspiration that had first fired him. This was in 1221, but neither the Brothers nor the Church approved it. Two years later he went to one of his hermitages far from Assisi, in Fonte Colombo, taking with him his devoted Brother Leo and a Canon Lawyer, and he rewrote the Rule to a juridical standard. This was approved by the Pope and the Brothers accepted it. This Rule is still followed by the Brothers today.

## Francis has a dilemma

In between all this wrangling and the composing of the Rules, Francis continued to travel and to preach, and to retire for weeks on end to quiet places to pray. He made many natural hermitages in the wooded hills of Umbria and Tuscany. These prolonged times of prayer became his source of strength to continue. It was in times like this that Francis was unsure if God really wanted him to continue preaching, seeing that he experienced so many graces in his prayer. So he asked his Brothers:

"What do you think, Brothers, what do you judge better? That I should spend my time in prayer or that I should travel about preaching? I am a poor little man, simple and unskilled in speech. I have received a greater grace of prayer than of speaking."  Bonaventure Maj. Leg.

And he continued to tell them about all that God was doing for him when he prayed. Then he thought about Jesus, who held back nothing of himself for himself, and went about preaching to people about God's fatherly love for them. Anxious to be sure he was doing the will of God he decided to send two of his Brothers to consult first, Brother Sylvester, who was praying continuously in the mountain above Assisi, and then to Sister Clare and her Sisters who prayed continually at San Damiano. They were to ask God what Francis should do: devote himself to prayer or to go about preaching. In a very marvellous way the two Brothers came back from their errand with the same conclusion: both Brother Sylvester and Sister Clare agreed that it was God's will that Francis should continue to preach.

## Francis founds the Third Order

So it was that his fame spread far and wide as he went around proclaiming the kingdom of God and preaching peace. He urged the crowds who flocked to hear him to leave their sinful lives. He did not mince his words either as he urged men and women to cut out their faults. He feared no one's criticism, but spoke the truth clearly and boldly. His honesty and his enthusiasm for the Lord drew people from every class of society: the well-educated and distinguished, the poor and the lowly – all were amazed by his words. Those who were single, both lay and cleric, sought to join his Lesser Brothers, the First Order of St Francis; virgins and widows entered monasteries to take on a life of penitence. Under the guidance of St Clare, many of these monasteries became the Second Order. Those who were married also begged to be able to live the kind of life he put before them as so desirable, so Francis gave them a Rule and a habit and called them the Third Order of Penitents. They lived in their own homes and did wonderful deeds of charity wherever they lived. They prayed regularly and fasted too. As the numbers grew they formed small local communities which met once a month for prayer and sharing. Today this form of life still continues and is called the Secular Franciscan Order.

**Francis and the animal world**

The best known thing about St Francis is his way with animals and birds. Francis had a real kinship with all of nature, both animate and inanimate. He regarded everything he saw as his brother or sister. In the Canticle of the Creatures which he wrote when he was blind and sick He marvelled at the radiance of Brother Sun; he praised the precious beauty of Sister Moon; Sister Water was humble and useful. In the presence of animals and birds he was fearless. He saw himself as created by God, just as they were. It seems that he was so much at peace within himself that the creatures sensed it, and were in no way threatened by him.

The most amazing of these stories is about a fierce wolf which for a long time had harassed the town of Gubbio. It not only ate the livestock, but killed some of the townspeople as well. Francis took pity on them, and protected only by his faith and the sign of the cross, went out of the city to encounter this wolf. It lost no time in rushing towards him, jaws wide open. Francis did not run from it. He just stood there, made the sign of the cross, and called for it to come to him. To the surprise of the people who were watching from a safe distance, the wolf went up to Francis and lay down! After haranguing the wolf for all its misdeeds, he got it to promise to stop harming the people of Gubbio, and in return they would feed it every day. The wolf showed its compliance by putting its paw into Francis' hand. So Francis led it back into the town, and got the people to agree to feed it. Then he gave them a great sermon about turning from their sins, and to fear hell more than the wolf! The people were very happy and they praised God for sending Francis to save them. From then on the wolf went round the town every day and the people fed it, until it died two years later of old age, to the great sorrow of the townspeople.

There is a famous occasion when he preached to a group of doves and jackdaws. Surprised that they did not fly off he told them to praise their Creator and love Him, because he gave them feathers, wings and a constant supply of food. He even touched them and they did not go away until he blessed them and gave them permission to go. Another time some swallows were making such a din that the people could not hear what Francis was saying, but when he asked them to keep quiet, they did. Animals seemed to have no fear of him. He freed a rabbit from a trap, and it stayed with him; he returned some fish caught in nets to the water. So close was he to everything God created, and so humble within himself that is was not power over creation that he sought. It was kinship. The animal world seemed to sense this and welcomed him as their Brother. It is not for nothing that he is now the patron saint of ecology.

## Francis' personal austerity

It seems strange to our age and culture to discover how hard Francis was on himself and his body. He allowed himself no 'comfort zones' such as we cling to! When he was young his body had caused him to sin through greed and pride and all the other temptations the young experience. It must be said, however, that none of his biographers accuse him of sexual misconduct. After his conversion he was determined to avoid sin at all costs. It has to be remembered that he was Italian, and passionate about everything he did. He was very conscious of being tempted to lust, so much so, that one day, when it was snowing, he went out and built seven mounds. He then spoke of them as if they were persons:

> "Here, the larger one is your wife; those four over there are your two sons and two daughters; the other two are a servant and a maid who serve them. Hurry then and get them some clothes because they are freezing to death! But if the complicated care of them is annoying, then take care to serve one Master!"

That 'little exercise' cured his lust that day! However, he was always wary of the company of women, and in his Rule of 1223 he 'firmly commands' the Brothers not to have anything to do with women which might cause suspicion. He did not seem to trust men's ability to control their sexual desires because he didn't trust his own!

He was most frugal with his food, and it is said he never ate anything hot. He went in for long fasts. Once, he spent the forty days of Lent on an island, and took with him only one loaf of bread. When they went to fetch him, they found he still had half a loaf uneaten.

He would sleep on the ground, with a rock for his pillow. His clothes were meagre and worn and patched. If he met a beggar who was more poorly clothed than he was, he would swop his clothes for the beggar's. It is not surprising that he fell ill so early on in his life and died at the age of forty-four. However, he did have the grace as he was dying, to apologize to Brother Ass, as he called his body, for treating it so badly!

## Miracles

People in the Middle Ages were always on the alert for a miracle. So as the holiness of Francis became widely known through his travelling around preaching, those who were sick began to approach him. In a place called Toscanella a man had only one son who was a weakly child and could not walk. He was still sleeping in a cradle. The father asked Francis to come, but he refused, because he thought he was not worthy of such a power. In the end the importunity of the father won the day and Francis went. He prayed and laid his hands on the boy, blessed him and lifted him up. The boy then stood, immediately healed and started to walk around the house.

In Narni there was a man called Pietro who was

paralysed. He could only move his tongue and blink his eyes. He sent word to the bishop to get Francis to come to visit him. When Francis got there he made the sign of the cross over him from head to foot, shoulder to shoulder, and Pietro was immediately restored to health.

There is another touching story about a woman of Gubbio who was very crippled. She approached Francis and showed him her hands, begging him to touch them. He had great pity on her and did so. Her hands were immediately healed. So she went home full of joy. She made a cheesecake with her own hands, and offered it to Francis. He took just a little of it, and then told her to go home and eat the rest of it with her family.

There are hundreds of miracles recorded that took place through Francis, both before he died and after he died, but today we do not give them so much importance as they did in that time. They were, as Francis well knew, done by the power of God. He was just God's instrument.

## 'CHRISTED'

### Francis is sick

Francis' long travels in Italy and abroad, the harshness with which he treated his body, the extreme poverty which affected his clothes, his food, his housing eventually took their toll on his health. While he was in North Africa he had picked up an eye disease which gradually grew worse. He suffered continual bouts of fever, probably malaria. His stomach was ruined. When in 1918 his body was disinterred, they discovered tuberculosis in his bones. By 1224 he was a very sick man, but he would not give up either his preaching or his praying.

## Christmas at Grecchio

His growing weakness did not prevent him meditating imaginatively on the great mystery of the Incarnation and the birth of the Son of God. In mid-December 1223 Francis walked south, about thirty-five miles, to the mountain Friary at Grecchio. He knew a gentleman there called John Velita, to whom he said: "I would like to celebrate the next feast of the Redeemer with you. I would like to recall his birth in Bethlehem in order to see all the poverty that he endured from his birth to save us sinners."

Francis instructed him to put a manger filled with hay in a cave on the mountain and to bring there an ox and an ass. Here he and his Brothers and the farmers who lived around came on Christmas night. There was an altar where the priest said the Midnight Mass. Francis, though not a priest, was a Deacon, so it was he who sang the Gospel story and preached the Good News. Everyone was filled with such joy that the hills and the trees around rang with their song. They caught this joy from Francis, and ever after people have made 'cribs' at Christmas time.

## How Francis acquired a mountain

Ten years earlier, when Francis and Brother Leo were preaching in the Spoleto valley below Assisi, they passed by the castle belonging to Orland di Chiusi, a very rich man. There was a feast going on in honour of a young knight who had just been invested, and a big crowd had gathered in the hope of a meal. Francis jumped on a wall and clapped his hands for attention. Then he sang them romantic Troubadour songs to entertain them, and having got their attention, preached to them on the need to endure the discomforts of this life for the sake of the life to come – just as Jesus had told his disciples: *You will have pain, but your pain will turn into joy.* Leo recalls that Francis' words were so powerful that the people were rapt in attention. The Count too had heard the sermon and afterwards asked if he could talk to Francis about the salvation of his soul. But Francis told him to go back to his guests and give them his attention. After the meal they would talk. The upshot of this episode was that the Count offered to give Francis a mountain, which was now abandoned, 4,000 feet high in Tuscany, called La Verna. Francis, who never wanted to own anything, had longed for somewhere right off the beaten track where he and his Brothers could retreat to pray. So when the Brothers who were sent to look at it, said it was ideal, he accepted it gratefully. The contract was sealed verbally. Only after Francis' death were documents drawn up.

## Francis receives the stigmata

La Verna became a very important place for Francis in 1224. It was his custom to go on retreat for about forty days in preparation for the feast of St Michael on 29 September. In this year he walked the sixty miles or so, mostly uphill, to his mountain hermitage. He took with him Brother Leo and a few Friars who would ensure that he was not disturbed. All his life he had sought to follow the crucified Christ, and now, through pursuing this journey, he sought an even closer intimacy with his God. As he prayed alone on this mountain he was more than usually aware of God's presence, and he was filled with joy. He wanted to know what more he could do to be conformable to God's will. So he took the Gospels, and after praying for guidance, opened the Book three times. Each time it was a passage from the Passion of Christ. So Francis understood that his dream of following Christ even to the cross was how God's will would be fulfilled in him. He wanted to experience the depths of Christ's love and the pain of his physical sufferings which were the tangible sign of this love.

Then, as he looked upwards, he saw something moving towards him from a distance. It drew nearer and nearer and shone with a great light. It was a Seraph with six wings. Two of his wings were raised upwards, two were over his head, as if for flight, and two covered the body of a man who was crucified in the centre of the Seraph. The vision filled him with great joy, as the man looked at him so graciously, but he could not understand what it meant. Then, as he looked down, he saw marks appearing on his hands, like the heads of the nails he had seen on the man on the cross. His feet too, were stamped with the marks of nails, and he had a wound on his right side which was bleeding. Now understanding came. In the words of St Paul: *I bear the marks of Christ in my body,* and *With Christ I am nailed to the cross.*

The desire to be one with Christ, formed when the San Damiano Crucifix spoke to him all those years ago, was now granted in its most vivid way. He was so touched by the immensity of Christ's love for his people as he experienced the way in which he suffered, that his first reaction was to write an amazing series of

I HAVE BEEN CRUCIFIED with CHRIST

"Then, as he looked down, he saw marks appearing on
his hands, like the heads of the nails he had seen
on the man on the cross."

statements expressing what God meant to him. It begins:

You are the holy Lord God who does wonderful things
You are strong. You are great. You are the most high.
You are the almighty King. You, holy Father,
King of heaven and earth.

There is no self-pity or indeed any thoughts about himself at all. He is immersed in the goodness of God, as he continues:

You are love, charity, You are wisdom,
You are humility,
You are patience, You are beauty, You are meekness,
You are security, You are rest,
You are gladness and joy.
You are our hope, You are justice, You are moderation,
You are all our riches to sufficiency
You are beauty.

The Praises of God 1, 2 & 4

This was the God he had shared with so many people in his lifetime of preaching. No wonder people caught his fire and that his vision renewed the Church.

### Francis, Mirror of the Passion of Christ

Yet at the core of Francis' extraordinary vision lies the great paradox of the Incarnation. In what he had seen in the Seraph he experienced Christ as transcendent, mysterious, God *and* a man, so of the earth that he could be hounded, tortured and murdered at the hands of his fellow men and not use his divine power to help himself. All his life Francis had continually pondered on how this man, Christ, related to God, his Father, in the midst of all this physical pain and suffering of spirit. His ponderings led him to the psalms, the actual prayers used by Jesus, to find in them those lines which expressed the attitude of one who is innocent, but who has been unjustly handed over to malefactors and rejected by the very people he loved. He had collected these lines into fifteen 'psalms' of his own. The collection became known as St Francis' Office of the Passion. His selection is based on words which the suffering Christ might have used to communicate with his Father at the time of the Passion and Death, and afterwards, at his Resurrection.

Jesus suffered in his life because he stood out in humility, simplicity and goodness against the traditions and ideals of the religious people of his day. He suffered without complaint and with great patience. Francis mirrored his Jesus in the same manner. He suffered physically, especially with his eyes; he was hard on himself in matters of food, sleep and clothes, more so even than Jesus! He suffered the rejection of his vision of Gospel living at the Chapter of Mats, and finally, on La Verna, Christ sealed him with the actual marks of the crucifixion. So lines from his *Office of the Passion* must have been often on his lips, such as these:

> You have driven my acquaintances far from me;
> they have made me an abomination to them.
> They repaid me evil for good and harassed me
> because I pursued good.
> I have been poured out like water
> and all my bones have been scattered.

All his life experiences had been lived in the light of the way Christ himself had shown him and in the strength of the love that the Passion revealed to him. His heart was always filled with that love and with the thought of Christ's suffering. He said: "We can boast in our weaknesses and in carrying each day the holy cross of our Lord Jesus Christ."

The desire to reflect Christ's love drove him to care attentively for his brothers and sisters and to have a humble disregard for himself. He is a true mirror of Christ as he lived and as he died.

## Francis composes the Canticle of the Creatures

Probably because he saw how great a privilege it was to be marked with Christ's wounds, he was very private about it. Very few saw them, even the Brothers closest to him. Walking became almost impossible, but being determined to carry on with his work, he rode on a donkey and continued travelling and preaching. Then his eyes grew so bad that he could not bear any kind of light, either sunlight or firelight. He retreated to San Damiano, where the Lady Clare looked after him and made him soft moccasins for his hurting feet. But he had to sleep in a kind of lean-to made of mats, by the convent wall, and was very troubled with mice that also lived there. It was dark in there, which was good, because his eyes were so bad and so painful that he could not bear the light of the sun, or even of the fire at night. He could no longer see the beautiful world around him, but it was at this time that he composed his *Canticle of the Creatures*, where he gives praise to God for Sun, Moon, Stars, Wind, Weather, Water, Fire and Earth.

These were his Brothers and Sisters. Even death for him was 'Sister Death'.

At that time the Bishop of Assisi and the Mayor had fallen out very badly, so much so that the Bishop excommunicated the Mayor. In revenge the Mayor told everyone not to sell or buy anything from the Bishop, or to draw up any legal document with him. Their hatred was huge! This upset Francis very much, especially as there was no one trying to reconcile them to one another. So he decided to compose another verse to his poem *The Canticle of the Creatures*. It goes like this:

> Praise be you, My Lord,
> through all who give pardon for your love,
> and bear infirmity and tribulation.
> Blessed are those who endure in peace
> for by you, Most High, they shall be crowned.

Then Francis sent one of the Friars to tell the Mayor – from him – to go to the Bishop's house, and take with him the city's magistrates and as many other people as he could. Next he asked two other Friars to go and sing the *Canticle of Brother Sun* to the Bishop and everyone who was there. He said: "I trust in the Lord that he will humble their hearts and they will make peace with each other and return to friendship and love."

It worked! First the Mayor, with tears in his eyes, apologized, "for the love of our Lord Jesus Christ and of his servant, Francis."

Then the Bishop said: "Because of my office humility is expected of me, but because I am naturally prone to anger, you must forgive me."

And so, with great kindness and love, they embraced each other, to the great wonder of the Friars and all who saw and heard it.

## Francis dies

Sister Death was very close. In 1226, two years after he received the stigmata, his illnesses grew worse. He asked to be carried to the Portiuncula where he had received so many graces. Even then he would say to his Brothers: "Let us begin to serve the Lord our God, for up to now we have done little."

Frequently given to melodrama, but never to draw attention to himself, he asked his Brothers to lay him on the ground, naked. This was for him a sign of total poverty and so that the devil would have nothing to hold on to should he attack in the last hour. Then he said to the grieving Brothers: "I have done what is mine to do; may Christ teach you what is yours."

The Minister General then brought him a tunic, a cord and underwear and said: "I am lending these to you as a poor man and you are to accept them with the command of holy obedience."

This Francis did, but he was glad that the clothes were borrowed and did not belong to him. He felt that he had kept faith with Lady Poverty to the end.

Lastly he spoke at some length to the Brothers about poverty and patience and keeping faith with the Church and with the Holy Gospel. Then, absorbed in the Lord, he died. It was the evening of 3 October, 1226. Even though it was twilight, larks gathered in huge numbers. They circled round the little hut for a long time, singing all the while. A beautiful farewell to their friend.

## Yet there is no farewell

There must be very few people in this world today who have not heard of St Francis. At his death, the undying lamp of his life, his values, his attitudes and the marvellous reflection of Christ's love that shines out from him, spreads everywhere. As we seek to save our planet, because it is the earth on which the Son of God walked, it is good to see in him the amazing respect and love he had for life, in people and the whole of Creation, and to follow in his way as we make our own journey to God.

# The Man Francis

What a man is before God,
that he is and no more.

*St Francis – Admon. XIX*

## Can we really know Francis, the man?

Thomas of Celano, one of the twenty-four early writers about the life and work of St Francis described the effect he had on the Church of the first quarter of the thirteenth century as a gleaming light. This, however, tells us more about those who experienced his charismatic presence and witnessed how the people responded to him, than the man himself. What everyone would like to know is what was he like as a person? Would it have been a good thing to have met him? Would I have liked to live with him and to have walked alongside him? Is he now so famous that he is out of my reach?

## His appearance

The first impression we get of new people in our lives is through what they look like, and it is fortunate that Thomas of Celano, has given us a description of Francis. Thomas was a friar who had lived with Francis in the early days, and so knew him well. He would certainly have been capable of telling us more exactly what he was like as a person, but the purpose of his biography was to give the church the image of the saint. This needs to be remembered when reading him. However, he does give us a pretty accurate account of what he looked like.

Francis appeared to Thomas as an eloquent man,

cheerful, kind, hard-working and humble. He then goes on to say:

> He was of medium height, closer to short, his head was of medium size and round. His face was somewhat long and drawn, his forehead small and smooth, with medium eyes black and clear. His hair was dark; his eyebrows were straight and his nose even and thin; his ears small and upright and his temples smooth. His voice was powerful, but pleasing, clear and musical. His teeth were white, well set and even. His lips were small and thin; his beard was black and sparse. His arms were short, his hands slight, his fingers long and his nails tapered. He had thin legs, small feet, fine skin and little flesh. 1 Celano XXIX.83

Pictures of him confirm some of these features, but the majority of them were painted after he had died, so we cannot be sure how good a likeness they are.

### The young man

There was nothing out of the ordinary, according to modern ways of thinking, about the way Francis lived until he was twenty-five. The son of a rich cloth merchant, he had access to plenty of money and the things money could buy. He loved to look good and his clothes were of the richest materials from his father's shop. Nevertheless, even here he showed himself to be eccentric, as he would put together all kinds of different stuffs, and would then put a sackcloth patch somewhere on all this finery!

Everybody loved him! The youth of Assisi flocked round him, and found him not only generous with his money, but fun to be with. He would play practical jokes; he loved to sing, and would lead the gang round Assisi with much noise and laughter. There were grand dinner parties and much carousing, thanks to his extravagance. Was he a Christian then? Thomas of Celano suggests only in name.

However, underneath all this brashness and joie de vivre was a kindly person, adaptable and affable. He was naturally courteous and rarely answered back brusquely. Even before his conversion he realized that because God had blessed him with good things, he should be generous to the poor. One day he was working in his father's shop and absorbed in serving his customer, when a poor man came in and begged alms, for the love of God. Francis took no notice of him, but later, when the beggar's words resounded in his memory, he realized how rude he had been in ignoring him, and resolved that from then on he would not deny a request to anyone asking for alms in the name of the Lord.

Later, for the same reason, he filled the dining table with loaves of bread, though there were only his mother and himself at the meal. When his mother asked the reason for this eccentric behaviour, he replied that it should be given as alms for the poor. This kind nature also prompted him to cheer up the prisoners in Perugia after the battle of Collestrada. He was particularly kind to a fellow prisoner whom all the rest marginalized.

At one time, in Rome, his preoccupations with the poor led him to exchange his rich clothes with one of the poor people begging outside the church, and in their place, beg for alms in French, which he loved to speak, though he could not do it correctly.

The young Francis, then, was an enthusiastic lover of the good life! He did everything with enthusiasm, passionately, and put his whole heart into whatever he did. Certainly, he was eccentric and dramatic. He never wished to draw attention to himself for his own aggrandizement but only to express how he felt sincerely and truthfully. For all his extravagant flamboyance there was a compassionate heart within him.

## Touched by God

Remember that day when he was with his usual friends and was suddenly struck motionless by an extremely strong grace from God, so that, as his friends saw, he was 'changed into another man'. Or was he? With the same wholeheartedness that he had thrown himself into a life of jollity and pleasure, he threw himself into the arms of the God who had so powerfully touched him. He was mocked and jeered at by his erstwhile companions, but just as he had been driven to seek his own pleasure before, so now he sought with his whole heart what he felt that God was calling him to do. As he had been ambitious for himself, now this ambition was changed into looking for a new way of living what God wanted, because that was what he wanted too.

On that fateful day when he went into the little church of San Damiano, God touched him again in a more particular way. As he gazed at the huge icon-like crucifix there, where Christ is portrayed as both crucified and risen, he was moved with compassion for this Poor Man. He had truly found 'the treasure' of the Gospel in the love that he realized that Christ had for him, by dying for him on the cross. Now he wanted nothing more than to be free to be with Christ. It was this love that drove him for the rest of his life as Christ's life became his life. He embraced it totally, so that later he would write:

> Hold back nothing of yourselves for yourselves,
> that he who gives himself totally to you
> may receive you totally!
>
> Letter to the Entire Order, 29

## His life-style

What immediately strikes the reader of the early Lives of St Francis is the way he was so very hard on himself. It has to be remembered that in the twelfth and thirteenth centuries and beyond, ascetic practices were considered a great mark of a holy life, but there was more to the way Francis treated himself. He was driven by his love for Christ to have nothing superfluous, even a small plate, in the place where they lived. He struggled with his natural love of food and good things by accepting whatever he could get when he went begging. Even if it were just scraps and looked awful, he ate it with gratitude. When he was invited out to dinner with a rich person, he would pretend to eat and hide what he didn't consume on his lap! He slept on the ground without a mattress, and often slept sitting up, using a stone or a piece of wood as a pillow. The story goes that once when he was ill he craved to eat a piece of chicken. When he got better he was so ashamed of his greed that he got a Brother to tie a cord round his neck and drag him through the whole city, crying: "Look! See this glutton who grew fat on the flesh of chickens that he ate without your knowledge." We think this is crazy, but the people were touched to the heart and were moved to better things because of this example. Such things went on all his life, so it is small wonder that his health had completely deteriorated by the time of his death at the age of forty-four.

None of these ways of treating himself was a gimmick or done out of a poor self-image. His only desire was to follow the Poor Crucified, as he called his Jesus. He wanted to imitate him, and to so school himself that there was nothing – no desire, no sin, no fault, no material thing, no person – that could get in the way of Christ's love for him, or his for Christ. This was life for him. All his drive and enthusiasm came from this. Before, in his youth, he had been driven by love of himself. He was a changed man, but not a different one. However, towards the end of his life he did apologize to his body – Brother Ass as he called it – for treating it so badly!

## Totally dedicated to compassion

The inspiration of Christ and the Gospel fired him to do even more for those who were in need than he had done in the past. This he did with great delicacy and sensitivity. One day he and his Brothers were sleeping, when one of them suddenly called out: "Brothers, I am dying! I'm dying of hunger!" So Francis woke them all up, ordered them to set the table, and bring what was in the place to eat, and water to drink, and he himself began to eat. He called all of them to join him, so that the hungry Brother wouldn't be embarrassed.

When he was preaching, which he did with great zest to many thousands of people, he was as confident as if he were speaking with a close friend. Each one felt he was speaking to them alone, which was a great gift. He put the same keenness when he was speaking to one person as he did to the thousands. Nevertheless, though he moved the hearts of his hearers deeply, there were times when he could not think of anything to say, and he would just give them a blessing. When he did speak he spoke boldly and with power, yet what he said was simple and so everyone could understand. He was obviously a gifted teacher, because he took into account not only what he wanted to say, but also the people to whom he spoke.

There is a lovely story about robbers which shows clearly Francis' understanding of human nature and his compassion for every kind of person – even thieves! The Brothers were one day arguing among themselves whether it was good to give alms to robbers – for some had come to them begging for bread. This was Francis' advice: they were to get some good bread and good wine, take them into the woods, spread out a cloth for the food on the ground, and call the robbers to come and eat. When they came, they were to wait on them joyfully and humbly. When they had finished eating they were to ask them to promise not to injure anyone – only that. The next time they were to bring them also eggs and cheese with the bread and wine, and when they had finished, say:

> Why do you stay here all day long, dying of hunger and putting up with so many hardships? When you do so many evil things, in will and in deed, you will lose your souls unless you turn to the Lord. It is better to serve the Lord, who will both supply your bodily needs in this world and save your souls in the end.     Mirror of Perfection 43

So because of the friendliness and humility which the Brothers showed the robbers, they listened and did everything they heard, and imitating the Brothers' humility, began to serve them by bringing them wood from the forest. Some of them even became Brothers themselves, and others repented of their past lives and promised to reform. This advice to the Brothers bears out Francis saying that he would not consider himself a friend of Christ unless he loved all the people Christ loved.

## How his love of poverty helped him to grow closer to God

It seems that he regarded his former love of really good clothes as an obstacle to receiving God's love, and he was keen that he and his Brothers wore simple clothes. He allowed them to have no more than two tunics, and these were to be mended until there was more mend than original! He did the same for himself. But if a Brother were ill, his compassion was stronger than his love of poverty, so he allowed him to have a soft tunic next to his skin, as long as rough and cheap clothing were on the outside. When he was travelling he would often give away his tunic to a poor man who had nothing, and would beg for clothes for the poor, especially when it was cold.

He wanted everything to sing of exile and pilgrimage. There was to be no room for extravagances. One Easter Sunday at Greccio the Brothers had set the table with a white cloth and glasses. Francis came down later, and when he saw this decorated table, he crept away, dressed himself as a beggar and called out for alms. The Brothers replied "Come in, man, for the love of him you invoked." Francis was given a bowl, and sat on the ground, saying: "Now I am sitting like a Lesser Brother!" He went on to explain how the example of the Son of God's poverty ought to be followed more closely than for other religious. Eccentric? Certainly. Dramatic? For sure. But such was the dedication of Francis to his ideal and his vision. It was his way of expressing a life that was full of meaning, and of love and peace.

## His attitude to women

Although there is nothing in the story of Francis' youth which indicates that he was involved with girls, being a young Italian, he was often tempted by lust. This is a perfectly normal phenomenon, but Francis dealt with it in his usual extravagant fashion. He would say wisely:

> "When one is too secure, one is less wary of the enemy. If the devil can hold on to one hair of a person, he will soon make it grow into a plank."

You remember the time one winter when he was tempted to lust and made those seven snow people? He took desperate means to overcome his sexual desires, but said it was the 'one Master' who helped him to overcome his lust; he would let nothing stand in the way of following Christ with every fibre of his body and soul.

There were two women, however, who were important in his life. One was the Lady Clare. He spent much time with her for about two years when she was about sixteen. He taught her what he had discovered about Jesus, so that she wanted to live like he lived. There was a real and genuine friendship of love between them. Later on, however, he was overly cautious. Once having established her and her Sisters at San Damiano, he would very rarely visit her. His Brothers used to chide him about this. However, when he was dying he received a note from Clare wishing to see him. She too was ill at the time, and as they were both in the same condition, a meeting was not possible. So Francis sent her a message to say that she would see him again, which she did after he had died.

The other woman was a certain Lady Jacoba de Settesoli. She was a rich widow who lived in Rome and was descended on her father's side of a Norman knight who had conquered Sicily. She had met Francis when he was in Rome at one time, and he had shared with her the love of God, and encouraged her to change her life. There was a strong bond between them. So much so that when he lay dying Francis said: "You know how faithful and devoted Lady Jacoba de Settesoli was and is to me and to our religion. Therefore I believe she would consider it a great favour and consolation if you notified her about my condition."

He further instructed the messenger – the quickest they could find – to tell her to bring with her cloth for a tunic the colour of ashes, and some of the little cakes she used to make when he was in Rome. A letter was written to this effect and the messenger about to take off, when a great commotion was heard outside the place where Francis lay. The messenger came rushing in to say that the Lady Jacoba had actually arrived. What should they do with her, seeing that women were not allowed in where the Brothers were? Francis answered: "I named her *Brother* Jacoba because of the strength of her virtue, so this command need not be observed in the case of this lady whose faith and devotion made her come here from so far away."

What was even more amazing was that she had brought the cloth Francis wanted and the ingredients for the cakes. She said she had become aware of the need to go to Francis while she was praying, and that she should bring these things. It seems that at the moment of his death he acted with his usual compassion towards both of these women and no one else.

## His joy

It might well have been that with all the harshness on himself he practised that he was a sombre, gloomy person as he lived his life the way Christ was showing him. That is very far from the fact. He insisted that joy was the great remedy against temptation. He embraced it as one of the gifts of the Holy Spirit. To anyone who felt sad or disturbed about something, he would encourage them to stay in the presence of God until they received once more the "joy of salvation".

On one occasion, when he was in Rome, he preached to the Pope and the Cardinals with 'such fire of spirit that he could not contain himself for joy' and actually began to dance as he spoke!

When he was experiencing a particular joy from the Spirit, he would break out into a French song of joy. Thomas of Celano himself saw him one day pick up a stick and put it over his left arm, while with the other hand he held a 'bow' bent with a bit of string, and as if he were playing a violin, he would draw the 'bow' over the stick, and again, sing in French a song about the Lord. He loved music and would sing whenever he got the chance.

There is a famous story about perfect joy that he asked Brother Leo to write down for him. It begins: "A messenger arrives and says that all the Masters of Paris have entered the Order. Write: this isn't true joy!" He then imagines all the bishops and archbishops near and far, the Kings of France and England have entered the Order; and that the Brothers have converted all non-believers to the faith, and that I have performed many miracles of healing. Joy is in none of these things. Naturally, Brother Leo asked: "Then what is true joy?" Francis replies: "Imagine this scene: I return here from Perugia (a town twenty-five kilometres from Assisi) in the middle of a freezing winter's night. There are icicles clinging to the bottom of my habit that cut into my legs. Freezing, I knock at the door and call out, and eventually a Brother comes and asks who I am. I reply 'Brother Francis'. He turns on me and tells me to go away. 'It is too late,' he says. I beg him again, but his comments get worse as he says: 'Go away! You are simple and stupid! Don't come back to us again! There are many of us here like you – we don't need you!' Then I say, in desperation: 'For the love of God, take me in tonight!' All I get is the stern reply: 'I will not! Go down the road and ask there!' And I hear his footsteps retreating. Brother Leo, I tell you this: if I had patience and didn't get upset in such a situation, true joy, as well as true virtue and the salvation of my soul, would consist in this!"

## His self-knowledge and humility

Many people recognized his holiness and would flock after him and praise him. However, he knew his inner weaknesses, especially his temptation to vanity. He once gave away his cloak to a poor woman, and immediately began to congratulate himself on his good deed. Then, just as quickly, he accused himself before those standing around of vainglory.

In one of his *Admonitions* he speaks of how he himself lived:

> Blessed is the servant who does not consider himself any better when he is praised and exalted by people than when he is considered worthless, simple and looked down upon, for what a person is before God, that he is and no more.
>
> Admonition XIX

These were the days when the behaviour of priests left much to be desired. He believed that he and the Brothers had been sent to help priests for the salvation of souls, and that they were to make up whatever was lacking in them. His great aim was to keep peace between them and the clergy, and to cover up their failings. When they had done this, they were to be even more humble.

His humility was at its height, however, when he received the stigmata two years before he died. He felt that it was such an honour to be marked with the wounds of Christ crucified, that he would not allow anyone to see or touch those wounds, except for those few who were looking after him. He never spoke of them nor did he feel proud to have been so graced. It made him silent in awe and praise, which is evident in those wonderful lines he wrote for Brother Leo immediately after that stupendous event.

## His love for the earth and everything on it

His way with animals was quite extraordinary, as we have seen. They seemed to understand what he said and obey him. He treated them all with great gentleness and found his God revealed to him in them. His affinity with the natural world was not an act. Behind it there was a deep theology – both he and they were created by God, and so they were brother and sister to him and to one another. He felt drawn to love all created things because of this and realized how necessary it was to have a genuine care for them all. They seemed to sense this inner peacefulness within Francis which sprang from his deep faith in and love for his Father-Creator. So not only were they not afraid of him, but were drawn to stay close to him. The following story is but one example of this:

> Once Francis was crossing a lake in a small boat. A fisherman offered him a little water-bird so he might rejoice in the Lord over it. The blessed Father received it gladly, and with open hands, gently invited it to fly away freely. But the bird did not want to leave; instead it settled down in his hands as in a nest, and the saint, his eyes lifted up, remained in prayer. Returning to himself as if after a long stay in another place, he sweetly told the little bird to return to its original freedom. And so the bird, having received permission with a blessing, flew away expressing its joy with the movement of its body. 2 Celano CXXXVI

ALL CREATION PRAISE GOD

The sun for Francis was Brother Sun, and the Moon, his sister, as was Water. Brother Fire had a great fascination for him, because he saw it as "beautiful and playful and robust and strong." He was even unwilling to extinguish lanterns, lamps and candles, because their brightness was a sign of eternal light.

He had a care for trees too, and forbad the Brothers to cut down a whole tree in order that it might be able to sprout again. He was particular about the Brothers' gardens. They were to leave some of it to grow wild to reveal the beauty of the Creator, but they were also to grow sweet smelling flowers for the enjoyment of those who saw them that they might be drawn to praise God. He would not even let worms on the road be trampled on, and would have bees fed in the cold of winter with honey and wine.

## Man of prayer

It has to be acknowledged that all these amazing characteristics of Francis were held together by his deep prayer life. From the time he first felt the touch of God he had realized that nothing would change, nothing would grow in him without the help and grace of God which he sought in constant prayer.

He had a great love for quiet places in the forests and hills of Italy where he would make himself little hermitages, and spend days on his own after a spell of preaching. He usually passed the forty days of Lent entirely in prayer, and frequently another 'Lent' round the feast of St Michael the Archangel. His prayer was very simple. You will remember how Bernard heard him pray all night the short mantra "My God and all things!" Few words, but a heart totally focussed on the God who loved him and all things. When he was with his Brothers, he would get up silently to pray, so that he would not be noticed. Nevertheless, the Brothers could not help seeing that he was changed in some way after his prayer, though Francis tried hard not to let others see the graces God had given him.

Francis left a few written prayers which show that adoration of the Father, the Son and the Holy Spirit was very important to him. Here is just one of his prayers of praise:

All powerful, most holy, most high, supreme God:
all good, supreme good, totally good.
You who alone are good,
may we give you all praise, all glory,
all thanks, all honour, all blessing and all good.
So be it, so be it. Amen.

Praises to be said at all Hours

He loved Our Lady and dwelt on her relationship with each Person of the Trinity. He describes her as:

Daughter and servant
of the most high and supreme King
the heavenly Father.
Mother of our most holy Lord Jesus Christ,
Spouse of the Holy Spirit.

Office of the Passion – Antiphon

Always a loyal son of the Church, he never failed to say the Liturgy of the Hours (The Divine Office). Wherever he was he would say this standing up straight and not allowing his eyes to wander. Like everyone else he was bothered by distractions, but got so used to turning from them that he called them 'mere flies'.

## His love of Scripture

It could be said that Francis was soaked in Scripture. His writings are a kaleidoscope of many texts that had sunk into his memory. Because books were expensive and in short supply, most of what he knew came from listening to the passages read in the Liturgy. He would mull over these and discover their deep wisdom for himself. It was in the Scriptures he sought to know not only God, but himself also. His sermons were impregnated with the words of scripture as he unravelled their mystery for his listeners with understanding and power. He never preached about things he had not discovered for himself.

## His foibles and his sickness

Francis' zeal for living the Gospel life and following in every way the Poor Christ would often lead him to excess. So keen was he that the Brothers should own no property at all, that one day, when he returned from a journey to the Portiuncula where there was soon to be a Chapter, he found that a large house had been built of stone and mortar. In a fury of anger that there should be in this place an example of wealth and comfort, Francis climbed up on the roof, and called some of the Brothers to join him. They immediately began tearing off the tiles and throwing them to the ground, intent on destroying the whole building. The knights of Assisi saw this and immediately called up to Francis that the house had belonged to the Commune of Assisi and not to him or his Brothers. Francis stopped what he was doing and replied that if the house belonged to them he didn't want to touch it.

While Francis was away on his travels to Egypt and the Holy Land, the number of Brothers continued to grow, and many of those who came were educated men and some were priests. They had a need to study and reflect if they were going to be successful preachers. This in turn necessitated having not only books, but a permanent place in which to do their work, with a desk and parchment and ink. They maintained that they could not function without these. To Francis this was a great threat to his vision of a poor and simple life, like Christ's, so he felt he had to resign his position as Minister General. Organization of such a large number of Brothers was not his strong point. All he wanted was to preach, to pray, and to live the simple life. In the end he had to accept that the needs of these new men had to be met.

His judgment of people was not always very accurate. On one occasion he sent five young women to St Clare as candidates for her Monastery. Clare said she would take four of them, but the fifth was not suitable. However, Francis insisted, and Clare obeyed him. In the end Clare was the better judge, as the fifth woman only lasted three months in religious life. It seems that feminine intuition was needed in this case!

As we have seen his greatest excess was in the way he treated his own body. During his last years he was a very sick man. He had contracted an eye disease in Africa which did not respond to the very severe treatment of the day. His digestive system did not seem to work properly at all. He was malnourished and frequently suffered from fever, probably malaria contracted first when he was a prisoner in Perugia. Deprived by his own choice of proper food, sleep and housing, it is no wonder he was such a physical wreck. But he would never give in to himself. Somehow he had to force his body to follow the dictates of his spirit. In all these sufferings he showed heroic patience.

Moreover, he never expected his Brothers or anyone else, to go to the same extremes. He encouraged them to sense and moderation!

Towards the end of his life his eyes were so bad that there was only one remedy: cauterization. He was in a panic about the pain that he foresaw was inevitable, so he prayed that Brother Fire would, in the power of its Creator, temper its heat so that he might be able to bear the pain. His prayer was answered, because afterwards he praised God because he had, in fact, not been troubled by any pain!

## Francis writes

People in the Middle Ages were not nearly so reliant of pieces of paper and writing as we are today, but there were important occasions when it was necessary, so, as we have seen, when he was a lad Francis was taught to write, in Latin, by the Canons of the Cathedral in Assisi, who had a small school for boys. They learnt to read in Latin from the psalms, which is probably why Francis was so familiar with them. Much can be learnt about him as a person and even more about his dreams and ideals from the things he wrote. In Francis' case you find in his writings just what you have met in the events of his life. He is a man of great integrity, and his focus is always on Christ as he is in himself and Christ in the whole of creation. So many events in his life show his compassion for people and for animals, but the most touching piece of his writing is in this letter, which he wrote to Brother Leo, his priest-secretary, about the time of the Stigmata, when he wanted to be left alone:

Brother Leo,

Health and peace from Brother Francis!

I am speaking, my son, in this way – as a mother would – because I am putting everything we said on the road in this brief message and advice. If afterwards, you need to come to me for counsel, I advise you thus: In whatever way it seems better to you to please the Lord God and to follow His footprint and poverty, do it with the blessing of the Lord God and my obedience. And if you need and want to come to me for the sake of your soul or for some consolation, Leo, come.

Letter to Brother Leo

There is a collection of short writings called *The Admonitions*. In one we see his amazement at the presence of the Lord in the Eucharist. He writes:

Each day he himself comes to us, appearing humbly, each day he comes down from the bosom of the Father upon the altar in the hands of a priest!
Admonition I

There is another Admonition which gives the clue to the means by which Francis lived life to the full. It begins:

The apostle says: "The letter kills, but the Spirit gives life." And it ends: "Those people are brought to life by the spirit of the divine letter… who by word and example, return every letter to the most high Lord God in whom every good belongs."
Admonition VII

All his writings reveal just how much he lived by the spirit of the Scriptures. He knew whole passages by heart, and could weave different bits together to bring out his message. He wrote two letters to the new members of the Third Order, the Brothers and Sisters of Penance in which he had decided to explain to them "the words of our Lord Jesus Christ, who is the Word of the Father, and the words of the Holy Spirit, which *are spirit and life.*" Speaking of prayer in this letter he says: "And *day and night* let us direct praises and prayers to him, saying: *Our Father, who art in heaven...* for we *should pray always and not become weary.*" So you can see how easily the words of Scripture flow in and out of his writings so naturally.

It is in this letter that we are given a glimpse of his excitement when he thinks of the relationship God forms with those who seek and find him:

> O how glorious and holy and great to have a Father in heaven! O how holy, consoling, beautiful and wonderful to have such a Spouse! O how holy and how loving, gratifying, humbling, peace-giving, sweet, worthy of love, and above all things desirable it is to have such a Brother and such a Son: our Lord Jesus Christ.
>
> Second Letter to the Faithful

This is the only time in all his writings where he allows himself to use the explosive "O!".

His concern in the Church is for priests to have great respect and reverence for the Blessed Sacrament, and he does not mince his words in trying to correct those who are careless:

Are we not moved by piety at these things when the pious Lord puts himself into our hands and we touch him and receive him daily with our mouth? Do we refuse to recognize that we must come into his hands? Let us, therefore amend our ways quickly and firmly in these and all other matters.                                   Letter to the Clergy

Considering Francis' absolute dedication to a life of poverty, it may not come as a surprise to discover that he wrote in his first Rule: "Let none of the brothers, wherever he may be or go, carry, receive, or have received in any way coin or money... not for any reason, unless for an evident need of the sick brothers." He has another rule which says: "Let it not be lawful for [the] Brothers to ride on horseback unless they are compelled by sickness or a great need." Like Francis, until he was too sick, they walked everywhere!

One of the most touching letters he wrote was addressed to a Minister (a Superior in one of their houses). This man had experienced some hostility and opposition from someone in his community and was in a state about it. Francis gently says that he must consider "as a grace all that impedes you from loving the Lord God and whoever has become an impediment to you... even if they lay hands on you." He goes on to say that he must love his persecutors, and must not wish they be better Christians. Then comes something which shows the heights to which Francis himself would go in such a position, when he continues:

I wish you to know in this way if you love the Lord and me, His servant and yours: that there is

not any brother in the world who has sinned –
however much he could have sinned – who, *after
he has looked into your eyes*, would ever depart
without your mercy, if he is looking for mercy.

Letter to a Minister

In addition to the two Rules, he wrote praises to God,
for Our Lady and quite a few prayers, most of which
appear within other writings. He centred his prayer
on praise and adoration of the Blessed Trinity, and
was imbued with the goodness of God in all things.
We can listen to the awe in his voice as he prays:

All-powerful, most holy, Almighty and supreme God,
Holy and just Father,
Lord King of heaven and earth
we thank you for yourself,
for through your holy will and through your only Son
with the Holy Spirit
you have created everything spiritual and corporal,
and after making us in your own image and likeness,
you placed us in paradise.

Then, as always, he recognizes the reality that is in us,
for the next line is:

Through our own fault we fell.

Earlier Rule, Ch. XXIII

Some time during the year in which he died, Francis
wrote a *Testament* in witness of his own life. He writes
of his vision for the Brothers who had gathered
around him – well over 5,000 by 1226. The tone of
this writing is firm and strong. He seems confident
about the way he has lived. There is a strong

recognition that everything hinged on God leading him to a radical conversion when he 'went among lepers' and all the bitterness of his life changed to sweetness.

The strength of his commitment to the Church stands out as he professes his loyalty to her priests who consecrate and distribute the Body and Blood of Christ, which was always his central devotion. Not blind to the fact that many priests were not what they should be, he does not let this stand in the way of what of his respect for what they have been ordained to do for the Church and for him. He wrote two strong letters to the Clergy about the need for care and respect for the Blessed Sacrament. Similarly his life-long love and respect for the words of Scripture is stressed as he explains how he used to gather up any he found on scraps of paper and put them in a suitable place.

He was absolutely certain that his vocation and those of the men who had joined him, was to live the Gospel in poverty, according as the Lord had given him to speak and write in the Rule. For this reason he was committed to work to avoid idleness and give a good example. His certainty was confirmed because the Pope had approved his plans.

The strength of his desire to obey could not be put more strongly than when he says: "I wish to be a captive in the hands of the Minister." He is anxious that the Rule be kept and not altered in any way, and that those who do not keep it be disciplined severely. Everything must be done "in a more Catholic way".

## The man who loved life

Francis' exuberance for life in all its aspects sprang from the Good News about the love God has for everyone and everything he has created. Francis embodied that love in his compassion for the people in his life and for all of creation. He was captivated by God himself, but always in the context of the world in which he lived. Christ, the Son of God, had lived and loved within our world, and shown us how to be truly human and truly devoted to his Father. So Francis became more and more the person that God had created him to be. Thus he was able to draw people to the same orbit of love and commitment to so good a God.

## Our original questions

Perhaps now it is possible to answer those questions with which this chapter began. Would it have been good to meet him? Yes, undoubtedly. To see and hear him preach would have captivated anyone who was there, just as the Lady Clare and Lady Jacoba were held by his explanations of the Gospel. To meet him face to face would have been even better, because of that knack he had of making everyone feel that they mattered to him by looking into their eyes.

To live with him would be another matter! It would be almost impossible to live up to his high ideals or to imitate his way of growing in the spirit by being excessively tough on the body. His lack of organization would drive some people crazy, as would his long hours of prayer when he would be 'unavailable'. The dramatic way in which he would act and react would have been slightly nerve-racking. It would be irritating to watch him give away his cloak or his tunic to someone less fortunate in cold weather than he and be unable to stop him. On the other hand, there would be times when he was great fun; his joy and his peace were infectious. To hear him singing the old troubadour songs as he used to do when he wanted the attention of a crowd, would have raised our spirits. However, it would not have been possible to get close to him, because for all his going out to others, he was a very private person. The inner core of himself was truly given over to God, and no one would want to usurp that place.

His first Brothers walked alongside him and were carried away by his zeal. Later Brothers found his way too radical and criticized him openly. To go along peacefully with him a person would have to be truly sympathetic to his vision, ready to make allowances and prepared to be endlessly patient with his unpredictable ways. On the other hand, one would have benefited immensely from his enthusiasm and his genuine love.

Is Francis then out of our reach? Can we only admire him from afar? To a certain extent, yes. He is very much The Saint, whose ways are beyond our ways. Nevertheless, he has much to share with us, principally the way in which he allowed Jesus to captivate him and give him life. Like him we can grow into the same kind of compassion he had for others. We would do well in this materialistic age to understand how our love for things can be an obstacle to our fidelity to God, as Francis did. In these violent days, his message of peace is one everyone needs to hear and work towards. True, we may not be able to be as deeply committed as he was, but there is much to be thought about as we see the wholeheartedness and honesty with which he threw himself into the way God was leading him.

## Truly known only to God

There is a story in the *Little Flowers of St Francis* connected with the time he received the stigmata. Brother Leo heard him pray thus:

> Who art Thou, sweetest God? And who am I, a wretched worm, thy worthless servant?

To the end of his life he was still marvelling at the two biggest mysteries of life – God and himself. He would only have found the answer to these two questions on that 4 October, 1226, when God revealed himself to his Poverello. Francis the man, Francis the Saint, Francis the beloved of God – all are one and the same.

## Litany of St Francis

This Litany sums up both the man and the Saint that Francis grew to become. It also offers a chance to ponder on his life and his gifts, and to capture something of his spirit. The opening four lines are taken directly from the way he wrote about God and about Our Lady.

God the Father, most high and most glorious
God the Son, Word of the Father
God the Holy Spirit, the Paraclete
Holy Mary, Mother of our Most Holy Lord Jesus
St Francis of Assisi
Obedient Son of the Spirit

Francis, true lover and imitator of Jesus
Follower of the Poor Crucified
Man of faith

Poor man of God

Bringer of peace

Lover of all Creation

Loyal servant of the Church

True Brother of Jesus

True Brother of all Friars Minor

True Brother of all Poor Sisters

True Brother of the marginalized

True Brother of the Sun, Wind and Fire

Model of humility

Model for the sick and the blind

Seeker after chastity

Lover of the Infant Jesus

Lover of the Eucharist

Lover of the Cross

Lover of penance

Dwelling place of the Most High

Witness of God's love for us

Man who longed for martyrdom

Man of the Spirit

Man of contemplative prayer

Man of joy

Generous man

Example of trust

All things to all people

Preacher of the Word of God

Francis, patron of ecology

Francis, loved by all people

Francis, protector of birds

Francis, friend of animals

Francis, little man of God

Francis, compassionate man

Francis, full of the praises of God

Francis, the Mystic

Francis, marked with the wound of Christ

Francis, in glory.

## Prayer by St Francis, from his Letter to the Entire Order

Almighty, eternal, just and merciful God, grant us in our weakness the grace to do for you alone what we know you want us to do and always to desire what pleases you. Thus inwardly cleansed, interiorly enlightened and inflamed by the fire of the Holy Spirit, may we be able to follow in the footprints of your Beloved Son, our Lord Jesus Christ. And by your grace alone may we make our way to you, Most High, who live and reign for ever. Amen.

# Ambition for Love
# The story of St Clare

Love Him totally,
who gave Himself totally for your love.

*St Clare*

## PREPARATION
### The light begins to shine

It was early summer in the year 1193. The morning was cool as the sun rose across the Spoleto valley, and glinted onto the roof of the Cathedral of San Rufino. The piazza was in shadow as a shawled lady walked slowly towards the door. The Lady Ortolana was heavily pregnant. She made her way to an altar where Mass was about to begin. After the Mass the expectant mother stayed on, looking earnestly at the crucifix above the altar.

"My Lord," she prayed, "I beg you to protect me from the dangers that face me when I give birth to this child. Keep us both safe and help me."

She stayed there a while, and as she waited, still praying, she seemed to hear a voice telling her:

"Do not be afraid, woman, for you will give birth in safety to a light more clear than light itself."

Ortolana felt much comforted by this reassurance, and returned to her home next to the Cathedral. Sometime in July her prayers were answered, and she gave birth safely to a fair-haired girl. She did not delay to have the baby baptized. She called her Chiara (Clare in English). This name, which means 'brilliance', recaptured what the voice had said to her earlier, but only she knew its prophetic significance.

Clare's full name was Chiara di Offreduccio. Her father, Favarone, a tall, fair Lombard, every inch a knight, was often away from home. In fact, as he does not feature in her story it is thought that he died before she was of marriageable age. He was a member of the *maiores,* the aristocrats of Assisi, as opposed to the *minores*, or the merchants and the poor. Her mother was descended from the royalty of France. She had strength, courage and determination in her blood, which took her on arduous and dangerous pilgrimages, to Mount Sinai and the Holy Land. Nearer to home she journeyed to Rome, and to San Michele de Monte Gargano in south Italy. She was accompanied on these journeys by the young Pacifica di Guelfuccio, who lived just across the piazza from the Offreduccio house. She later said that Ortolana went on these travels "for reasons of prayer and devotion". The arrival of her first born put an end to this kind of devotion. Two years later Catherine was born, and finally another girl, Beatrice.

## First steps in faith

Now Ortolana's task was to bring out similar faith, prayer and devotion in her daughters. The young Clare took readily to this kind of education. As a small child she would count her prayers with pebbles. At meal times, when much rich food was served, she would secretly get one of the servants to take her helping out to the poor who frequented the steps of the Cathedral next door. She soon discovered that in those days physical penances were an accepted way to holiness, and though she had beautiful clothes to wear, underneath she wore a garment made of such coarse cloth as the servants wore. Like all young noble ladies, she did not go out and about, except with her mother to visit the poor and minister to them. Nevertheless she had a high reputation in the town for piety, and was esteemed by all who heard of her.

## Evacuation to Perugia

In 1199, when Clare was about six, all the nobles, including the Offreduccio family, fled to Perugia from the revolt in Assisi of the poor against the rich. There she made friends with Filippa di Ghislerio d'Alberico and Benvenuta of Perugia, both of whom would became life-long friends. The nobles of Assisi then persuaded the men of Perugia to wage war against Assisi, and in 1202 the famous battle of Collestrada took place in which the young Francis fought and was taken prisoner.

## Christ is her choice, not marriage

At last peace was made, and in 1205 the Assisian nobles returned home. Clare was twelve by then. She spent the next four years with her family, praying with them, and visiting the sick and poor with her mother. She learned how to read and write – in Latin, of course, as it was the language of the church. She achieved a high standard of both. It is said that her written Latin was better than Francis'! Like all young aristocratic women of those days, she acquired the arts of sewing and weaving, which were to come in so useful later on in her life. She must also have prayed much on her own, as it was at this time she began to be drawn to Christ in a very special way, so that when the idea of marriage cropped up, she wanted nothing to do with it. Even now, her love was drawing her to Christ and not to any husband. She grew more beautiful every year, and there were many young men who wanted to marry her. One of these, Lord Ranieri de Bernardo of Assisi, was refused by Clare many times. She would not even listen to him, and told him roundly that he should despise the world! When she knew what she wanted, or did not want, she was a very determined young lady. Her parents wanted her to marry someone great and powerful, as she herself was from a noble family, but she held firmly to her integrity.

## Enter Francis

The proximity of her home to the Cathedral was to play a significant role in her life. One Sunday, instead of the usual priest giving the sermon, a young man, rather scruffy looking, but with dark eyes burning with enthusiasm, climbed into the pulpit. From what he said Clare suddenly saw a totally new picture of the Jesus to whom she was so drawn. The young man made him so human, so understanding, so humble, and yet in complete control of his situation in a quiet sort of way. She drank in his words, and longed to hear him speak again about the Gospel. She could hardly wait for the following Sunday. There he was again! He fired Clare and the whole congregation with new ways of looking at well-known Gospel stories.

Who was this person? Where did he come from? Why was he so poorly clad? Clare asked around her friends, the servants, anyone who could tell her. She soon learned he was Francis Bernadone, whose father owned the fabric shop. This young man had, in the last four years, changed from being the jovial leader of the local youth into a penitent. What is more, he was inspiring several young men to live as he did. Clare didn't care what he looked like. She only saw in him something she was yearning for herself: a deeper knowledge and awareness of Christ, and a way in which she could become more involved with her God. The difficulty was how was she to meet him to have a private conversation.

## Vocation becomes clear

Francis, however, had heard about Clare's reputation for goodness. So he made the first move and went to visit her. Clare, of course, was surrounded by her family in the house, and there was little chance of privacy, so this time she took the initiative. With Pacifica's sister, the Lady Bona, she went very often to meet Francis secretly over a period of almost two years. Her mother, apparently, knew nothing of this, and no one stopped her. Her desire to learn more and more about Jesus, and Francis' gift of making him live for her were worth everything to her. He set her on fire with his words and his deeds, and she did not need much persuading to understand that for her the 'world' and its values held no hope of happiness and all the attractive things in it would not satisfy her. At these meetings both had a companion, for Francis took with him Brother Philip, who also spoke persuasive words to her. Once Francis had told her all he could it did not take long for Clare to become sure where her vocation lay. She had a clear insight that only a close union with Christ would satisfy her, no matter what it cost. She accepted that Christ's words *"Go sell... give to the poor... Come, follow me"* were life for her. All she needed now was the opportunity to do what the Gospel spoke to her.

## PROBATION
### Palm Sunday, 1212

Now it was time for practical arrangements to make possible the gift of herself to God alone. The first thing she did was to sell the land that was part of her inheritance, and while she did this, she also sold part of her sister Beatrice's portion too! The money realized she gave to the poor. This caused much anger in her family, not only that she gave away the proceeds, but also she had lowered the value of the rest of the land by breaking it up by the sale. Regardless, she made plans to leave home. It was the end of Lent in 1212. On Palm Sunday, dressed in her finest red dress, she went to Mass in the Cathedral. All the noble families were there, including many of her friends.

When the time came for the people to receive their palms, everyone went up to the altar, except Clare, who remained alone in her place. She stood there, calm and recollected, and just waited. When all the palms had been distributed, to the amazement of them all, the Bishop himself walked down the aisle and gave her a palm himself. She smiled at him, and solemnly they made a slight bow to each other. What was the meaning of this extraordinary happening? Was the Bishop giving her a sign that he knew what her desires were and what she was planning to do and tacitly giving her his consent? Possibly, because Bishop

Guido and Francis were friends and the Bishop had helped Francis in many ways.

During that day Clare did everything normally, concealing with difficulty her mixed feelings at the prospect of leaving her family. She was sad to be leaving her mother and her sisters without saying goodbye to them, and excited by the prospect of being united with the One she loved above all. When everyone had gone to bed, still dressed in her finery, she stole downstairs, not to the main door which was guarded, but to a special door at the side of the main door, commonly known as the Door of the Dead. It was barred with wood and stone, but some extraordinary adrenaline enabled Clare to shift the barriers and get out into the dark, narrow street on the opposite side to the piazza. She made her way to one of the gates that was being repaired, and so no impediment to her going, as a locked gate would have been. So off and away she hurried as best she could in the dark the four or so miles, down the hill, across the fields, and into the woods. There Francis and his Brothers greeted her warmly in the little church of St Mary of the Angels.

So Clare joined the Brotherhood of Francis. She exchanged her fine dress for a poor tunic of coarse material, which Francis gave her, and made do with a rope for a belt. Then Francis cut her long fair hair in a round, and gave her a veil for her head. She, then, placing her hands in the hands of Francis, vowed herself to God and became a true Penitent, one who was about to change her life and life-style completely for the love of her Lord. This, indeed, was the only 'marriage' she sought.

CLARE JOINS FRANCIS

*"So Clare joined the Brotherhood of Francis…*
*Then Francis cut her long fair hair in a round…"*

## To the Benedictines at San Paolo

Now Francis obviously could not let her stay there with the Brothers, who in any case slept rough in huts in the woods, so he and Brother Philip set off with her for the great Benedictine Monastery of San Paolo. They arrived about two in the morning, and Clare was taken in and next day put to work as a servant. She was not asking to become a nun there. They were exceedingly rich; she wanted only the poverty of the Poor Christ. On this first day of Holy Week, she was setting out to follow the pattern of Christ's life, so that she could be more closely united with him.

Trouble began almost immediately. When her Uncle Monaldo, then head of the family, discovered she had left her home, had sold her patrimony and had refused to make a good marriage which would have increased the wealth of the family and brought them honour and power, he gathered his relatives and off they ran to storm the Monastery in protest. There they tried every means they could to get her to return home: they used violence, evil advice, enticing promises, saying that no one had done it before in her family and she was letting them down by becoming working class. At this point Clare took 'sanctuary' by holding on to the altar and whipped off her veil to show her tonsured head, which was an accepted sign that she belonged to God. Frightened though she was, she was determined not to be taken away from the service of Christ. The violence of her relatives grew, and in proportion, so did her strength, her love and her determination. She would follow what she had learned from Francis about humility and poverty and suffering persecution. Eventually they gave up and went off.

## To Sant'Angelo – Catherine comes too

However, the Benedictine life was not what she sought, so after eight days – that is, in Easter Week, she was taken by Francis and Philip to another place higher up Mount Subasio called Sant'Angelo. A group of women lived there in community and prayer. It was here that her sister, Catherine, aged about 15, left home and joined her, saying she too wanted what Clare wanted. Once again the Uncles came with even more violence. They knew that they had lost the battle with Clare, so they tried physical force this time and tried to drag Catherine away by the hair! Catherine yelled out to Clare for help. But Clare knew that she could do nothing herself against such men. But God could give Catherine what she could not, so she prayed. Suddenly Catherine became too heavy for all of them together to lift, and as one of the uncles raised his arm, ready to strike her, it became paralysed. After that the rest of the relatives left, giving the victory to the two girls. Catherine and Clare were reunited and hugged each other with great joy. When Francis came soon after, he cut Catherine's hair in a round. Like Clare, with her hands in the hands of Francis, she too vowed her life to God, and Francis renamed her Agnes. Now there were two, they could set up house themselves, so Francis took them to the little church of San Damiano, at the bottom of the hill, below the city of Assisi. It was here that he directed them in the way of the Lord.

## To San Damiano

Clare felt at last she was settled. She was not put off by the smallness of the place, nor by its isolation. San

Damiano was well outside the city walls. Soon the reputation of the two sisters spread and others began to join them. First was Pacifica, who had gone on pilgrimage with Ortolana, Clare and Agnes' mother. She knew the two sisters well. Then came Benvenuta from Perugia, whom Clare knew from the time they were evacuated. After that Cecilia joined them from nearby Spoleto, and after her Benedetta, who would become the next Abbess after Clare's death. Four years later came Filippa, another of the *nobilitas* of Assisi, and another friend of Clare from days in Perugia. Over the next ten years Balvina, Christiana, another Agnes and another Benvenuta gave themselves to Christ under the leadership of Clare. In 1226 her mother, Ortolana came and three years later her youngest sister Beatrice followed their mother. By 1238 there were fifty Sisters, whose names appear on a document concerning the sale of some land.

## Clare's charism – Simplicity and Poverty

What drew all these women to Clare's way of life? Undoubtedly it was first and foremost the enthusiasm, joy and peace of Clare herself. She was like a magnet with the charism to draw others to Christ through her own total dedication, her prayer and her humility. Her way to Christ was through poverty. To be truly poor, to have no desire for power, or things, or reputation or anything or anyone other than Christ, meant that there was room in her heart for God and all his abundant gifts, above all, his love. This spirit was catching and life-giving.

For the everyday needs of the Sisters Clare relied on God to provide. Most monasteries, for example the Benedictines, were at that time extremely rich in land and money. Clare wanted nothing of that, so in 1216 she asked Pope Innocent III for an extraordinary thing: she wanted to have a special permission, or a privilege – a private law – to own absolutely nothing. This was unheard of – to live without property or a set income, but as it was an ideal clearly set out in the Gospel, he granted it to her, seeing that her trust in God was so great. And that is how they lived.

## Miracle of the oil and the loaves

There were two friars who lodged in a hut outside the Monastery, one was their chaplain and the other went begging for them. There were also Sisters who went begging too, and the generosity of the people of Assisi was not lacking. There was one occasion when there was indeed a real need. There was no oil, and there was nothing of seasoning for the sick. So Clare washed the jar and put it in the usual place where the Brother who went begging for them would find it. When they called him, he came running as he knew the need was great. When he found the jar, much to his annoyance, it was already full! He grumbled and said: "These women have called me to make fun of me, since, look, the jar is full!" Clare had obviously not only washed the jar, but prayed, knowing that the Brother would be concerned for the welfare of the sick Sisters.

On another day the time came for their meal. There was only one loaf in the house. Half of this had been given to the Brothers. Clare told Sister Cecilia to cut fifty large slices off the other half! She grumbled about it being impossible, but nevertheless did it, and in fact everyone had a good slice of bread, just as

Clare had predicted! Her trust in God's providence was never unfounded.

Clare herself sums up the kind of life they led together in these early days when she wrote in her Testament:

> When the blessed Francis saw that although we were physically weak and frail, we did not shirk deprivation, poverty, hard work, trial, or the shame or contempt of the world – rather we considered them great delights... he greatly rejoiced in the Lord.

## Daily life

Soon after this Francis wrote for them a Form of Life in which he simply encouraged them to live according to the perfection of the Holy Gospel. They trusted the insight of Francis, and became firmly rooted in the Gospel of Christ, with their hearts bonded to the Holy Spirit as they served and loved their heavenly Father. When she was still young and full of energy Clare set the way to do this. She shirked no menial task; she washed the beds of the sick Sisters; she fetched water from the well; she served the others at table; she washed the feet of those who had been out begging.

There was one occasion when, as she washed the feet of a Sister, this Sister accidentally jerked her foot and caught Clare's mouth. Clare took no offence, and carried on washing and drying the offending foot, and ended by kissing it. It seems that no one ever forgot this little incident. At night she would see that they were well covered and would wake them gently for the Night Office. Above all she was an inspiration

SISTERS
TOGETHER

*"She shirked no menial task*
*she washed the beds of the sick Sisters...*
*she washed the feet of those who had been out begging."*

to their prayer. When she came from the chapel her face radiated joy and peace, and she would share with them what she had gained from the Lord.

### Francis orders Clare to become Abbess

In 1215, three years after they had gone to San Damiano, there was an important Council of the Church, the Lateran Council. Among many other things they decided that there were to be no new

Rules written for monks and nuns. Those who wanted to start another religious family had to choose from one of the four already existing, of which the Benedictine Rule was the most popular. Seeing that this would cause a difficulty for his Sisters, Francis ordered Clare, very much against her will, to be the Abbess at San Damiano, in order that she could be ready to be recognized by the Church. Probably Francis had in mind that Clare should accept the Benedictine Rule which required an Abbess. It was very important not to deviate from the Church's requirements on account of there being so many heretics who rebelled and were excommunicated.

## Clare and penance

Clare was twenty-one at this time, and in the fervour of her youth, practised penance to excess. She ate nothing at all on Mondays, Wednesdays and Fridays, slept on a bed of twigs with a stone for a pillow, and always wore a hair shirt. Francis was anxious for her, but was well acquainted with her strong will! So he asked Bishop Guido to go with him and together they ordered her to eat something every day. She obeyed, but what she ate was only an ounce and a half of bread, and a glass of wine, if there was any. In those medieval days penance was the best way in which Christians, women especially, sought to please God, but when she was dying she said:

> Once I came to know the grace of her Lord Jesus Christ through his servant Francis, no pain has been bothersome, no penance too severe, no weakness, has been hard.

*Life of Clare*, Ch. XXIX:5

97

## A problem of Rules

Until 1218 the Sisters lived with no specific Rule, except to live by the Gospel. There were many groups like them, and Pope Honorius III wanted to tidy things up in case he would have to support all these women. So he asked one of his Cardinals, Hugolino, to provide them all with the same Rule, so that they could come under the umbrella of the Church. He gave them the Benedictine Rule, together with a Form of Life written by himself, which told them how to live it. It was very strict and rigid. Because Clare and her Sisters were obedient to the Church they had to accept it and live it as best they could. Clare was upset because there was nothing in it about poverty, or community, or work. Luckily she had her Privilege of Poverty; she had the small Form of Life Francis had written and she still had the two friars to look after their spiritual and material needs. In spirit, she was certainly still a Franciscan.

## Hunger strike

In 1220 Cardinal Hugolino spent Easter at San Damiano. He really enjoyed being there, and a letter he wrote afterwards expresses his happiness to be in the company of Clare. Seven years later he became Pope Gregory IX, so in 1228 Clare requested and received a renewal of the Privilege of Poverty, which some other monasteries which were following Clare's way also asked to have. However, in 1230 a big change took place in the Pope's relationship with Clare. After the death of Francis the Friars had asked him to sort out some of their problems in following the Rule that Francis had left them, and the upshot of it was that the Pope forbade the friars to minister to the Sisters without specific permission from him. Clare, to whom the Word of God was spiritual food and drink, said, politely, to the Pope that if he took away the chaplain, she would not have the Friar who went begging for them either. She virtually went on hunger strike! When Pope Gregory heard this he softened his original edict, and said that Brothers could go to the Sisters, provided they had the permission of the Minister General. Clare's quiet determination had once more prevailed.

## Death of Francis

Four years before all this, in 1226 Francis had died. Clare was devastated. She cried out in her distress:

> Father, O father, what shall we do? Why are you abandoning us poor women? We are forsaken! To whom are you entrusting us? Who will comfort us in so great a poverty, poverty of merit as much as of goods? You, who were so often our help in times of distress!          1 Celano 2 Ch. X 116

The Brothers carried his body to the Sisters. When they saw him, and saw the marks of the stigmata on his body, they were inconsolable. Clare felt like a boat without a rudder, and totally alone, except for the vision they had shared together. This was, perhaps, the greatest poverty she experienced in her whole life.

# PERFECTION

## Clare gets sick

Clare was now travelling up the steep way of the Cross, the only way to perfection in the kind of love with which she knew that God loved her. Pope Gregory (Hugolino) did not continue his former friendship. Her health had been poor for the past two years, and now, in 1227, she began to be really ill. She became so weak that she had to be lifted in her bed to sit up. Nevertheless, this was perhaps the most fruitful part of her life. In her bed she refused to be idle. She would spin thread and weave cloth which the Sisters made into purificators and corporals, which they gave away to the local parishes. There must also have been many long hours on her own, and she who had served the Sisters with so much love and energy, now had to endure being totally dependent on them for her needs. She did not complain and never referred to her illness to others outside the monastery. All the time she was ill the Sisters said she did not relinquish her habit of continual prayer and her relationship with God deepened.

## Clare writes to Princess Agnes of Prague

It was at this time, 1234, that she first wrote to Princess Agnes of Prague. Agnes was the daughter of King Premysl of Bohemia (modern Czechoslovakia). In those days (the early thirteenth century) Bohemia was politically important to the balance of power and the wealth of Europe, and as was the custom, alliances were often made through marriages. At the age of three, Agnes was betrothed to another child, the son and heir of the Duke and Duchess of Silesia, but the boy died. Subsequently she was engaged to Henry, son of the German Emperor, Frederick II, but he also died. The English Henry III also asked for her hand, but she refused him. In the end she was officially betrothed to Frederick II himself.

Then she discovered Clare. When she learnt from some Friars who had recently arrived in Prague that Clare's chief aim was to live according to the Gospel and serve the poor Christ in poverty and humility, she enthusiastically answered: "This is what I wish and desire with all my heart."

So with the help of Pope Gregory IX she got herself released from her engagement to Frederick. She gave away all her riches by building a hospital for the poor and a monastery for the Sisters and another for the Friars. On 11 June 1234 she entered the monastery, together with seven other Bohemian ladies. She was twenty-three, and quite inexperienced in what was expected of her as a Poor Sister. So she wrote to Clare in Assisi for advice. That is how the correspondence and the friendship began.

Four of the letters Clare wrote have survived, and in them she shares with the young Agnes many of her thoughts about poverty, humility, prayer and following the poor Crucified Christ. She and Agnes never met, but corresponded until just before Clare died in 1253, when she wrote for the last time. By then a real bond of friendship had grown between them. These letters are centred on Christ and the love he showed by dying on the cross, so Clare writes:

> … be strengthened in the holy service of the poverty you have begun, out of the burning desire of the Poor Crucified. For us he suffered the passion of the Cross.　　　　　First Letter

Her roots in the Gospel are everywhere apparent. She says of Christ:

> The fox has its lair, and the birds of the air nests, but the Son of Man – that is to say Christ, had nowhere to lay his head, but bowing his head he gave up his very life.    First Letter

Central to her encouraging advice to Agnes, and something she learned from Francis, is the closeness of God to the heart of the faithful person:

> Neither heaven nor the rest of creation can contain the Creator; only the faithful soul can be his dwelling place and his home, and this comes about only through love.    First Letter

She teaches Agnes to pray by *gazing* at Christ, by *placing* her heart and soul in him, and by desiring him above all things. Agnes certainly benefited from Clare's advice, but Clare too must have gained insight into her own relationship with God through sharing it with a like-minded person.

### The Saracens' attack

It was while she was ill that tragedy hit the convent. The Saracens (Moslems) invaded the enclosure of the Monastery, and the Sisters were in danger of being robbed and raped. Clare, sick though she was, got out of bed and called for the Blessed Sacrament, which was kept in a silver pyx enclosed in an ivory box to be brought to her. She prayed fervently: "Lord, I beg you, defend these your servants whom I am not able to defend at this time."

Suddenly, she heard the voice of a little child: "I will always defend you."

The Moslems' bravado suddenly disappeared, and they slunk away. The following year they returned, this time to besiege Assisi itself. Clare was distressed. She called her Sisters and said, "Dearest children, every day we receive many good things from that city. It would be terrible, if, at a proper time, we did not help it, as we now can."

She asked that ashes be brought and that the Sisters remove their veils. First she put a lot of ashes on her own head, and then on the heads of the Sisters. She told them to go and pray to the Lord for the liberation of the city. By the next day the whole enemy army had disappeared, never to return.

## Miracle of hearing

The Christmas before she died Clare was, as usual in those days, confined to her bed. At the time of Matins all the Sisters went to the chapel, leaving her alone. Clare was upset and frustrated that she could not be present at the Christmas services. She sighed and said to the Lord, "Lord God, look, I have been left here alone with you."

Then as she listened out for the singing of the Sisters below her, she heard instead an organ and the singing of the whole Office of Readings sung by male voices. It was the Brothers who were singing in the church of St Francis at the other end of the town. It was as if she were actually there! It is in connection with this story that she is now the Patroness of Television!

## Clare, Mirror of the Passion

When you think that Clare spent the first twenty or so years gazing at the crucifix in the chapel at San Damiano, it is not surprising she was so clear about the meaning of Christ's Passion. A kind of light shines out from the centre of his body on the people standing near. His eyes are open wide, looking out. His face is serene. He is very much alive! This cross captures the whole of the Paschal Mystery – the passion, death AND resurrection of Christ. It was during the twenty-seven years of illness that Clare deepened her love for the Crucified Christ, when she herself was asked to accept not being able to DO anything. She would gaze at him, and see there all the love he had for her and the whole human race, and she would lose herself in his suffering love. One Holy Week she lost count of time from the evening of Maundy Thursday, when she began contemplating Christ's agony in the garden, until the following evening, Good Friday. She experienced the effect of his sadness and pain. It was a blessed time for her. On the Friday evening a Sister had to rouse her from her prayer so she could eat something, as Francis had ordered her to do. Clare told her not to tell anyone what had happened. She was very private about her relationship with her Lord.

The Passion of Jesus, for Clare, became the symbol of his 'highest poverty', a phrase she often used to describe the kind of poverty she wanted to live in imitation of him. He left all the 'riches' of heaven to come into our world, and in the end was rejected by his own people and lost his very life. She realized, as did Francis, that right in the midst of this poverty – this death – comes the great power of God. There is no other resource. God raised Jesus from death. He lives now a transformed, but still human, life, beyond human death. Into his poverty came the greatest richness imaginable: life, in its highest essence, pure, vibrant, full and utterly fulfilled. It seems that Clare cannot just see Jesus suffering and dying without also seeing that in the midst of this poverty is THIS life. So she speaks of the 'delights' of the Passion, and of 'his riches and honours which last forever', but can find no words to describe them exactly. It is the power of life and love that Jesus' passion, death and resurrection brought which both Francis and Clare mirrored in their lives, and it brought joy to all around them. That is why they can be called passionate lovers of life.

Clare wrote to Agnes of Prague, early on in their correspondence:

> If you suffer with him, with him you shall reign;
> If you weep with him, with him you shall be joyful;
> dying with him on the Cross of affliction,
> you shall possess mansions in heaven
> in the splendour of the saints.
>
> First Letter

Far from being a morbid dwelling on pain and distress, it is a cry of hope and an invitation to her friend to commit herself totally to the Poor Crucified. How was she to do this? Not so much by practising physical penances, as by enduring patiently all the vicissitudes that came her way, as Jesus had done.. Clare's most powerful witness to this was the way she endured those twenty-seven years of sickness, when by nature she was such an active person. This was her way of being transformed into the likeness of Christ and of giving him love for the greatest love he reveals by his passion and death.

## Miracles of healing

Clare was so deeply rooted in the self-emptying she had learnt from Francis and from looking at Christ crucified, that she became a channel of the love and healing power of Christ. The author of her Life sums it up thus:

> The beloved Crucified took possession of the lover
> and she was inflamed with such love
> of the mystery of the Cross
> that the power of the Cross
> is shown by signs and miracles.
> In fact, when she traced the
> sign of the life-giving Cross on the sick,
> sickness miraculously fled from them.

Many of her healing miracles took place among the Sisters in the community. Sister Balvina was cured of an abscess on her breast. Sister Christiana was healed of deafness, and Sister Cecilia of a cough. Clare did not search round the community to see who needed healing. Often she would wait, even for years, as she did with Sister Benvenuta, who had lost her voice for almost two years before Clare signed her with the sign of the cross and she could speak properly again. She knew her Sisters well, and they had caught from her the value of bearing all things patiently so as to be closer to the sufferings of Jesus. In all, she healed nine Sisters of various complaints. On one occasion she healed five Sisters who were sick at the same time with various things. She usually did this through making the sign of the cross on them, saying some words which the Sisters could never quite catch. Whatever they were, they were effective prayer. Surely her own closeness to her Crucified Lord made her a channel of his healing power on which she could draw whenever there was a need.

Before she herself was sick, many people from the city would also come to see Clare with their problems. There was Mattiolo, a little boy of five or six, who had a pebble up his nose! Every effort had been made to get it out, to no avail, and the boy seemed to be in danger. His mother brought him to Clare who made the sign of the cross over him, and the pebble fell out! On another occasion St Francis sent her Brother Stephen who was very mentally disturbed. After she had signed him with the cross, this Brother went to sleep for a while in the place where Clare usually prayed. When he woke up, the Sisters gave him something to eat, and he went back home cured!

Not only was she concerned with physical sickness but was also on one occasion that we know of, acted in the capacity of a Marriage Guidance Counsellor! She brought together a knight who had been separated from his wife for twenty-two years. He had always been adamant that he would never have her back, even when good people told him he should! Then he got a message from Clare who said he had to receive her back immediately, and she told him he would become the father of a son who would bring him great joy. And so it was! Everyone received the help they needed.

## The Rule problem is resolved

Pope Gregory IX was succeeded by Pope Innocent IV, and in 1247 he gave Clare and the many other Monasteries which were following her way of life, a new Form of Life. This was a vast improvement for her, because at long last the Pope placed her in the care of the Minister General of the Friars Minor. She could consider herself truly Franciscan now, but not completely so because there was nothing in it about owning nothing. Once more she politely complained, and after a short time the Pope withdrew his Rule, and more or less said "Do what you like"!

This gave Clare the opportunity she had been wanting for a long time: to write her own Rule! She was the first woman to do so. She based it largely on St Francis' 1223 Rule, but she also incorporated what was useful from the other Forms of Life that had come her way. She certainly had her own ideas, too, having lived the life for almost forty years! The Rule reveals a woman who well understood the vagaries of human nature and how it can flourish in a Gospel oriented way of life. It was finished by 1251, and was approved by Cardinal Raynaldo, their Cardinal Protector. Besides the Rule and the Letters, Clare wrote a Blessing and a Testament in which she has all the Sisters who were to come in mind. She invited them to be faithful to Franciscan Poverty, and to become mirrors of Christ to each other and to the world.

## Clare dies

1253 came in and dragged on. Clare was very weak. She had been in San Damiano for forty years, and for the past twenty-seven of these she had been ill. Some time during this year she wrote to Agnes for the last time. In it she seems to be looking forward to being with the Lord in heaven, for she writes, adapting the words of the *Song of Songs*, thus:

O Queen of our heavenly King, may you, therefore, be inflamed ever more strongly with the fire of love!... and sighing, may you cry out from the great desire and love of your heart:

*Draw me after you,*
*let us run in the fragrance of your perfumes*
O heavenly Spouse
I will run and not tire, until *you bring me into the*
*wine-cellar,*
until *your right hand will embrace me* happily,
*you will kiss me with the* happiest *kiss of your mouth.*

Fourth Letter, 27-31

Not our language perhaps, but it is not difficult to sense her excitement at coming at last to the end of her journey and to be safely in the arms of God.

Early in August, Pope Innocent IV with some of his cardinals went to visit her. How many dying nuns today would a Pope go to visit! Such was her closeness to the Vicar of Christ. He gave her the gift of perfect absolution and the grace of his fullest blessing. Clare was overjoyed that day because not only had she received Christ in Holy Communion earlier, and she had also seen his Vicar on earth.

On the evening of Friday, 8 August, Sister Benvenuta was sitting by Clare's bed with some of the others. They were softly crying as they saw she would soon leave them. Clare, meanwhile, was saying quietly to herself:

*Go in peace, because you will have a good escort.*
*The One who created you*
*has already provided you will be made holy.*
*The One who created you*
*has infused the Holy Spirit in you*
*and then guarded you as a mother does her littlest child.*

*May you be blessed, O Lord,*
*You who have created my soul!*

Process of Canonization, 11:3

As Sister Benvenuta continued to sit with her, she was thinking about the marvellous holiness of her Mother. Suddenly she seemed to see a crowd of virgins, led by one more splendid that all the rest, come into the room and approach Clare's bed. The virgin who was the greater covered Clare with a delicate, transparent cloth and bent low over her. Then they all disappeared. It seemed that Our Lady and some saints were preparing to welcome her into heaven.

On the Saturday when all the Sisters were gathered round, she reminded them all of many of the things she had taught them. She said her greatest desire was to have the Form of Life she had written confirmed by the Pope before she died. Finally, she made a good and beautiful confession. Sister Filippa said she had never heard anything like it. Clare made this confession because she thought she had offended in some way the faith promised in her baptism. This seems to hint that Clare had experienced spiritual darkness when God seemed to have deserted her, though apart from this phrase, there is no certain evidence for this. It would, indeed, be extraordinary for one so beloved of God not to have experienced the same kind of desolation Christ spoke of on the cross.

In her last hours she was much comforted by the presence of three of St Francis' first Brothers, now old men. She wanted them to read the Passion of Our Lord to her. Brother Juniper particularly filled her with joy, and she asked him if he had any new message from the Lord. To her his words seemed like burning sparks coming from the furnace of his fervent heart, and she was much consoled by them. Brother Angelo went round comforting the Sisters while Brother Leo could only kneel by Clare's bed and kiss it. He was grieving too much to say anything.

On 9 August, Pope Innocent IV who was staying at Perugia at the time, put his signature on Clare's Form of Life. A messenger brought it to her on the 10 August. Her prayer had been answered. She received the approval of *her* Rule before she died. She kissed the parchment roll many times and tucked it in the sleeve of her habit. So she could go forward in joy and peace and on 11 August, she was finally admitted to her reward – to be in the *wine-cellar* of her Beloved, united with Him for ever.

She was buried in St George's Church in Assisi and canonized in 1255 by Pope Alexander IV. Soon after her death the Sisters left San Damiano and moved into the city for safety. They are there to this day, faithful daughters of her spirit and her charism.

## Memories

What would the Sisters remember and cherish about their Mother after she died? They sent a letter round to all the Sisters of the order of San Damiano throughout the world telling them of Clare's death, and in it said that they were without *their leader, venerable mother, and teacher*. Prominent in their minds was her long prayer and contemplation. To them, this was outstanding, and from this was evident the great love she had for the Lord. In her illness, not only did she continue praying, but always patient, she never complained about her physical problems nor about having to be cared for by the Sisters. This was quite hard for her, as she had always been the one to serve them. They had experienced how her heart still went out to them when they were in trouble, just as it had when she was young and healthy and would weep with them as she identified with their problems. To them she was both serious in her dedication and full of joy at what the Lord was doing in their lives. They wholeheartedly agreed with the way in which she signed her Testament as their *Mother and servant*. This was how she always was – someone who loved them, and like Christ therefore, served them, often in the most menial ways. Even when she was sick she always had their welfare at heart.

Sister Filippa would recall how Clare would confide in her, and how she once told her about an amazing dream she had when she climbed a high stairway to St Francis. Sister Angeluccia would tell of the day when the heavy door fell on Clare which took three friars to lift off her, and she was unhurt. Sister Cecilia remembered the day Francis sent five ladies to join them. Clare had said that one of them was not suitable, but Francis insisted. Clare was right in the end, and that one only stayed a few months.

Of course, they all remembered the big things, like the miracles, but also the small things, such as when the cat brought a towel to their Mother's bed when there was no one else around. They remembered the mystical things, like seeing the Child Jesus standing by her on two occasions. Above all, perhaps, they remembered her total integrity, purity and holiness. They compared her to Our Lady and could not find adequate words to describe all that she meant to them.

Let Clare describe herself in her final words:

*In the Lord Jesus Christ, I admonish and exhort all my sisters, both those present and those to come, to strive always to imitate the way of holy simplicity, humility and poverty and to preserve the integrity of our holy way of living... And loving one another with the charity of Christ, may the love you have in your hearts be shown outwardly in your deeds.*

Testament, 56

# The Woman Behind the Light

This woman was the first of the poor,
the leader of the humble.

*Papal decree of Canonization*

## Her name foreshadows her deeds

When that baby girl was safely delivered to her mother, Ortolana Favorone, in 1194 in Assisi, she was baptized Chiara or Clare, 'the clear one'. It was, indeed, a prophetic name, one on which Pope Alexander IV delighted to play in his Decree of Canonization in 1255. He begins thus:

Clare,
brilliant by her bright merits,
by the brightness of her great glory in heaven,
and by the brilliance of her sublime miracles on earth
shines brilliantly.

He continues in this way, a bit foreign to our ears, for another twenty-three lines! There is much truth in what he says, but our interest lies in what kind of person was she really. Who was the woman behind all that light?

Inspired by the Holy Spirit and encouraged by Francis, Clare was herself a light in her own world, by which many people saw the way to God. She set in motion a way of life so that many other women in their turn would become lights in the Church, through their living witness to God by being lovingly dedicated to him in poverty and prayer. They are now the world-wide family of the Order of St Clare, commonly known as the Poor Clares.

Pope Alexander IV, because as Cardinal Raynaldo, was Protector of her community, knew her well. In the same Decree for her canonization he appreciated the influence she had had all over Italy. By continuing the metaphor of 'light' he showed both how powerful this influence was and yet how gentle in touching people's hearts:

Yes, Clare hid, yet her life has come to light.
Clare was silent, yet her fame was proclaimed.
She was hidden in a cell, but was known in cities.
It should not be surprising that a light so enkindled,
so illuminating could not be kept hidden
without shining brilliantly
and giving bright light in the house of the Lord.

True though this was, it is advisable to remember that this was written to announce her place in the calendar of saints. When we read the medieval Life of St Clare, written precisely for her canonization, we are told of the marvellous things God did through her – the miracles, the life of harsh penance, the hours of prayer, the visions. The writer is not interested, as we are, in the saint's struggles on her faith journey as she travels through the minutiae of everyday life. He focuses on the finished 'product' – the Saint.

## The Process of Canonization

Is it possible then, after 800 years, to discover the 'person' of Clare that lies behind the portrait of 'the Saint'. It is most fortunate that on 24 November 1253, at the request of Pope Innocent IV, the Bishop of Spoleto, together with his archdeacon, Leonardo, and Jacobo, the archpriest of Trevi, met at the Monastery of San Damiano. Brothers Leo and Angelo who had been of the first close companions of Francis were there too, and a notary. They interviewed, under oath, fifteen of the Sisters who had lived with the Lady Clare. Later in the week they talked to two other Sisters. Sister Benedetta, who had been chosen as Abbess after Clare, told them that the entire community could testify to Clare's holiness. On 28 November, in the church of San Paolo in the centre of Assisi, they heard the evidence of the elderly knight, Ugolino di Pietro Giraldone. Clare had persuaded him to take his wife back after a separation of more than twenty-two years. In addition he told of how he had known her as a young girl, and was amazed at the holiness of her demeanour even then. Lady Bona was seen next. She spoke of the time she went with Clare to speak with Francis without her parents knowing, and how she had willingly listened to him and accepted what he told her. Lord Ranieri was one of the young men Clare had turned down in marriage! It is he who comments on her great beauty. A family neighbour, Pietro di Damiano, gave witness to her continual refusal to entertain the idea of being married. He knew she wanted to remain a virgin and live in poverty. Lastly, on 29 November, one of the family's house watchmen, Ioanni di Ventura, spoke of the rich lifestyle of the family, and how in the midst of it all, Clare would save her food to give to the poor. What convinced him of her holiness, however, was the number of miracles he knew about since her death that had occurred through her intercession. He had seen a mad man brought in ropes to Lady Clare's tomb and was immediately cured. This Process of Canonization is particularly revealing because it is a written record of the testimony of a great variety of people: fifteen Sisters who had lived at San Damiano with her and five lay people who had known her before and since she entered religious life.

These accounts are, indeed, rich. It is these who spoke of her humility as she served the Sisters; her patience in waiting for the Pope to grant her request for the Privilege of Poverty; her kindliness when any Sister went to her with a problem; her gentleness in correcting Sisters, and of her steadfast prayer and contemplation. They spoke of her abstinence and fasting, of how she refused all comfort. They told, with admiration, of her love of God and of poverty. Sister Filippa, perhaps conveyed most when she said, "Always she was happy in the Lord and never was she upset."

The Sisters always refer to her as Lady Clare. This was not for them a sign of rank, though she did belong to an aristocratic family, but it indicated the respect and affection they had for her. They did not call her Mother Abbess, or even Sister (which she herself preferred). She was, in fact, both to them, but it is obvious they preferred 'Lady Clare' from the number of times this name appears in the Process of Canonization.

### Her own writings

Clare did not leave any diaries or treatises on prayer or the spiritual life. She professed poverty, and parchment was very expensive. In fact, there are only six pieces of writing extant that were certainly written by her. There are the four letters to St Agnes of Prague which reveal most about her relationship with God; the Form of Life of the Poor Sisters, which is the Rule she wrote for them in the last few years of her life, and is still followed by the Poor Clare's today. There is also her Testament, which bequeaths to the Sisters the values she most wanted them to maintain after her death. Two other pieces are closely associated with her – a letter to Ermentrude of Bruges and a Blessing, but scholars are not certain that she actually wrote them, though they contain much of her thought, if not her style.

## Her enthusiasm

From a sympathetic reading of her Form of Life and her Testament it seems that Clare was an enthusiastic idealist. This is not to imply that she was demonstrative. On the contrary, her way of describing herself as *little plant of St Francis* would suggest she preferred to go unnoticed and to grow quietly in the shade of the man who had sparked her enthusiasm originally. Her way to follow what they discerned together was to love and imitate the Son of God, as Blessed Father Francis had shown her *by word and example.*

Her enthusiasm is evident when she recounts how her vocation was confirmed even before she knew it. Forty years after this happened, she recaptures the joy and freshness of Francis, shouting in French to a group of Italian peasants as he was rebuilding the little church of San Damiano:

> Come and help me build the monastery of San Damiano, because ladies will dwell here who will glorify our heavenly Father throughout His Holy

Church by their celebrated and holy manner of
life. Clare's Testament, 13-14

Forty years is a long while for someone to be
enthusiastic, and Clare carried it all that time because
of her love, not for an ideal, but for Jesus himself, and
through him, for the Father, who, she understands,
gave her her vocation every day:

> Among all the other gifts which we have received
> and continue to receive daily from our benefactor,
> the Father of Mercies, and for which we must
> express the deepest thanks to our glorious God,
> our vocation is a great gift.
> Clare's Testament, 2-4

That sense of gratitude and complete dependence on
God seems to be the root of her enthusiasm and of
her heroic courage and perseverance. When you
realize that the word 'enthusiasm' stems from the
Greek *'en theos'* which means 'in God', it is not
surprising that this is characteristic of Clare, for she
was intoxicated by God, as was Francis. Her
enthusiasm expressed her love for him through closely
imitating Jesus, in obeying the Gospel teaching and
in becoming a mirror for others, especially for her
Sisters. Surely this reveals tremendous self-effacement
on her part: she did not want to reflect herself, her
ideas, her power and authority, but only be a channel
for others to receive the love of Jesus. This 'mirror'
idea is her special mark of holiness and is what enabled
her to be so Church-oriented, broad in her view of
her vocation in and for the Church. She writes of
herself first as *'unworthy handmaid of Christ'* who
promises obedience and reverence to the Pope and

the Roman Church. There is nothing narrow or exclusive about Clare's approach to her God. So her love of her Lord leads in faith to utter loyalty and service. It gave her life and energy right up to the last hours of her death.

## Nothing – forever

The most outstanding way in which Clare's enthusiasm led her to follow after Jesus was the whole-hearted and total way in which she embraced *the Highest Poverty*. This was what had fired her to follow Francis' lead. He had heard the clarion Gospel call to *Go sell... and give to the poor*; to have no money, no haversack, no spare tunic, no shoes on the journey for Christ. Clare, too, found in this idea an invitation to total dedication to God. Perhaps it was the sheer practicality of Jesus' instructions that inspired their hearts. Here was something they could DO, for both were rich and comfortable in their homes. Once it was done and they both had nothing, they were anxious to keep it that way. Francis' last words to Clare were, "*Live always in this most holy life and in poverty.*" And Clare's to her Sisters were:

> Time and again we willingly bound ourselves to Our Lady, most holy Poverty, that after my death, the sisters, those present and those to come, would never turn away from her.
>
> Clare's Testament, 39

When she explains her ideal in her Rule you feel she is straining to find words adequate to encourage her sisters:

The Sisters shall not acquire ANYTHING as their own, neither house nor place nor anything at all; instead, as pilgrims and strangers in this world who serve the Lord in poverty and humility, let them confidently send for alms. Nor should they feel ashamed, since the Lord made himself poor for us in this world. This is the summit of highest poverty which has established you, my dearest sisters, as heirs and queens of the kingdom of heaven.                                    Rule Ch. 8:1-4

There, in the words she chooses, is her enthusiasm writ large! In the day to day living of this ideal she herself describes some of the qualities this poverty demanded. You can sense joy in what she says:

We had no fear of poverty, hard work, suffering, shame or the contempt of the world, but instead, we regarded such things as great delights.
                                    Rule Ch. 6:2

She acknowledged that the difficulties were real enough – the love she bore to Jesus did not take them away – but she did not allow them to assume any importance, so that she truly experienced the joy of the Holy Spirit. Nevertheless, she was a brave woman, one might well say daring, bold, to take on such a life in an age when money and riches were the values of the day and the poor were scorned, and to a large extent, ignored. They were a nuisance in the medieval world of material progress. It must never be forgotten that she was a daughter of that same medieval world and belonged to a rich upper class family. She could well have fulfilled her Christian obligation by saying her prayers and giving alms to the poor, as she had done in her youth.

That this was not enough for her is indicative of a generous spirit and openness to God. Once she had seen his Way, she goes straight along it, with the directness and simplicity of a child. Always a disciple of Francis, his simple words caught exactly how she wanted to live:

> To observe the holy Gospel of our Lord Jesus Christ, by living in obedience, without anything of one's own and in chastity.
>
> Rule Ch. 1:2

Unlike a child, however, she did not grow weary of the ideal of Gospel values. She had firmly promised to observe forever the poverty and humility of Our Lord Jesus Christ and of his holy Mother. It was no passing whim, but it did not come naturally or easily to her. She was in constant fear of her human frailty and weakness, prone as it was to every physical demand, so that she writes that time and again she had to re-dedicate herself to Poverty, to ensure that she would never give up.

Her enthusiasm, however, was of the tough kind. It grew into strong determination that no one, not even the Pope, would force her to deviate from 'having anything of one's own'. First she obtained from two Popes the 'Privilege of Poverty', a document which states that no one could oblige her or her Sisters to accept land, houses or goods. Pope Gregory IX once offered her possessions, fearing that he would have to take the responsibility for seeing the community fed and clothed. He was even prepared to release her from her vow. She strongly, but courteously, replied: "Holy Father, I will never in any way wish to be absolved from the following of Christ." Her fidelity to the Gospel life-style gave her the courage to stand up even to the highest authority.

## Serving Abbess

Why was she so reluctant to be an Abbess? Her humility was very real as was her idea of being faithful to Jesus, who washed feet. She had no aspirations to greatness or importance or power. She did not want to create for herself a little 'kingdom' where she would have sole rights and receive the obeisance of her Sisters, as did Abbesses in other Religious Orders. The true picture of her working out how to be Abbess in Gospel style is in her Rule, which she drew up after living it for forty years. She must many times have been describing what she had done, and what she thought important, when she outlined the role of the Abbess.

First of all, she saw herself as one of a family, where decisions about matters great and small are made with the Sisters. At the Community Chapters they would discuss and discern who should be allowed to join the Community; whether or not they should go into debt, who should be elected for responsible posts, and anything that concerned the general welfare and good of the monastery. She did not dictate; she shared her responsibility and authority. Like Francis, she sought to lead her Sisters, not by precept, but from the front, by example.

The most striking thing about the example she gave was her selflessness. She allowed herself no privileges, whether it were in her clothes – if a Sister had on a more patched habit than her own, she would immediately swop hers for it! In the refectory she would be the one serving the others. In the dormitory she would be the one to get the others up for prayer during the night. She expected nothing of her Sisters that she did not do herself, even to acknowledging and confessing her faults to them all. It would have been hard for a stranger to know who, indeed was the Abbess of this great house of prayer.

How then, did she carry out her duties, for she was not one to shirk her responsibilities? She ruled by love. She loved them all so genuinely that she hoped they would be inspired to obey her out of love. Again, it was the obedience of the family she sought, not that of fear or impersonal bureaucracy. She ruled with wisdom – that is to say, with her head and her heart. She must have exercised tremendous self-control, the result of continually turning to God and away from her self. We will never know how much she had to curb her feelings so as not to show that one Sister appealed to her more than another. She saw the harm it could do to have favourites, not only to the Sister herself, but also to the peace and unity of the whole community.

She ruled also with compassion. She was always the last refuge of anyone who was anxious or worried. How approachable she must have been. She herself wished the Sisters to feel so relaxed with her that they could

Act towards her as ladies to with their servant –
for that is the way it should be, that the Abbess
should be the servant of all the sisters.

Rule Ch. 10:4-5

She means here that the Sisters should feel so comfortable with her that they would share with her how they were feeling, and not stand on ceremony, as the lady of the house would relate to a well-loved servant. Only here, Clare reverses the roles: she is the servant, and the Sister the lady! She was, like a good servant, and therefore like Jesus, ever alert and sensitive to Sisters who were upset or disturbed for any reason. She would weep with them. Spend time with them. She did not always have a solution to their problems, but she always consoled them by being with them in their anguish. Because she was strong, yet sympathetic, she prevented many a Sister's distress from tipping over into despair.

If a Sister was sick, she was particularly solicitous that their needs were provided for. A motherly heart finds it easy to alleviate physical suffering by whatever means are to hand, but it is something special to remember that at such times a Sister may need counsel and encouragement, of either a spiritual or psychological nature. This Clare sought first. She saw the sick Sister as a whole person and never excluded her spirit while caring for her bodily needs. Although the Sisters kept silence most of the time, she encouraged them to speak with those who were sick to comfort them.

## Clare's relationship with her Sisters

So Clare followed in the footprints of Christ, the servant, and in every aspect of love for her Sisters, set a high standard for them. But never was her virtue such as to intimidate or frighten or seem beyond the reach of others. She carried it lightly and easily, however much it may have cost her, so that the Sisters were uplifted and encouraged by her. If she could do it, so could they. They were able to feel this all the more because Clare had a very genuine personal love for each individual. When a Sister went to her with their needs she must have felt that she was the only one who mattered to her. She did not betray their confidence, nor put them down when they were low, nor was she ever 'too busy' to listen to them. She wrote in her Testament (65-66).

> Let her (the Abbess) also be so kind and so available that all of them may reveal their needs with trust and have recourse to her at any hour with confidence, as they see fit.

However, her total availability to the Sisters and the humble respect she had for them must have caused its problems! She is not above appealing to the Sisters to ease her burden by remembering that in the end their vow of obedience to God does require them to do as she asks!

Such is an example of the gentle way she would admonish and correct her Sisters. She was keen that they should love and serve the Lord according to the highest Gospel standard, and, as every good mother does, she corrected them. She knew only too well by experience their human weaknesses and in the name of Jesus she urged her Sisters to fight against their pride and their envy, their greed and worldly worries. She would not have them speak ill of each other, grumble or complain. She did not tolerate arguing or trouble-making. It may be surprising that such faults arose in that community, but its members were made up of different classes and allegiances, so she was able to pin-point what had probably arisen in her Community. She had seen vanity and pride, envy and avarice, and Sisters full of anxiety about things. She had heard grumbling and criticism of one Sister by another. So she urges them to hang on to mutual love and respect, which 'is the bond of perfection.' Given that there were Sisters from both Assisi and Perugia, two places that were so often at loggerheads, it is not surprising that ill-feeling should arise from time to time!

## Her strength of purpose

A careful reading of her Rule, or as she calls it, her 'Form of Life', reveals a loving person of high ideals which are rooted in the ordinary things of convent life! It is written by a woman for women, but it is not fussy. There is a strong flavour to it. Further, her strength of purpose was revealed in her determination to remain loyal to Francis and what he had shown her. The Popes wanted her to adopt the Benedictine Rule, and indeed, imposed it on her for very many years, but in the end she prevailed. She not only borrowed from the Rule St Francis had composed for his men, but also persuaded the Pope to let the Franciscan Minister General be their official superior instead of one of the Cardinals. When it was a matter of anything interfering with her vision of how the Lord wanted her to live, she was fearless.

## Growth in God

Clare begins Chapter VI of her Rule by telling some of the story of her initial turning to God:

After the most High Celestial Father saw fit to enlighten my heart by his grace to do penance according to the example and teaching of our most blessed Father Saint Francis, shortly after his own conversion, I, together with my sisters, voluntarily promised obedience.

In this Chapter she states her clear intention to do penance. By this she means adopting a way of living that is continually turned to the Lord and not to herself. As we have seen in those days this often involved physical mortification that today has no meaning for us. Clare's biographer, and the witnesses for the canonization, all describe the extent to which Clare fasted and allowed herself no physical comfort. Nowhere in her writing does she so much as refer to such practices or put forward the value of them for others. It is almost as if she herself did not heed them. In fact, when she was close to death she said to Cardinal Raynaldo, a kind man,

After I once came to know the grace of my Lord Jesus Christ through his servant Francis, no pain has been bothersome, no penance too severe, no weakness, dearly beloved brother, has been hard.
Legend of St Clare 44

But here, in her Rule, she sums up her whole vocation as one who does penance for the love of her Celestial Father. She closely links this with the conversion of Francis, in such a way as to imply that her doing penance is also a conversion; not just something that happens once and changes your life, but something which goes on all the time, and continually changes you. To change is to grow, and growth is the sign of life. In Clare this change involved constant growth in becoming more like Jesus, who is the Life. It involved a continual turning to him in love and away from herself. Body, heart, mind and spirit Clare belonged to God. He could use her for whatever he wished: to remain hidden, to serve her Sisters, to counsel Popes, to suffer long illness and frustration. She hid in him so successfully that she is very difficult to find. Her very essence is contained in both hiddenness and availability. Perhaps Francis would say – humility, simplicity and love.

## Virginity and perseverance

In the Process of Canonization very many of the Sisters mentioned her virginity. They saw so much evidence of her union with Christ. Her desires were totally absorbed in him. She did not have to spell it out about penance because in such a way of life it is self-evident to those truly inspired by God *to observe the holy Gospel of our Lord Jesus Christ.*

As she draws her Testament to a conclusion she becomes wistful, and perhaps a little sad, because she realizes that there are and will be very few who will persevere in the highest standard set by the Gospels to keep to the straight way and pass through the narrow gate. If they do persevere then it is, as with every step on Clare's faith-journey, a gift of God.

> How blessed are those TO WHOM IT HAS BEEN GIVEN to walk that way and persevere to the end. Testament 73

She seems to understand how easy it is to just slip into mediocrity without being aware that it is happening. But she will have nothing to do with deliberate turning from the path, nor, interestingly enough, will she allow ignorance of the Gospel way as an excuse.

She signed off her Testament with a self-description that sums up her ideals: *I who am your Mother and Servant.* Added to that, one might say 'Mirror of our Lord Jesus Christ.'

## In the joy of the Spirit

The Rule of St Clare and her Testament are, as it were, public documents. They were written not only for her contemporary Sisters, but for all "those to come", as she often tells us. They contain the map of the route she followed to God, as well as revealing her own priorities.

We are also privileged to a much more intimate sharing of the desires and passions that drove her out onto that Way in the four letters extant that she wrote to St Agnes of Prague. They were written over a period of about the last twenty years of Clare's life, the fourth letter being sent in 1253, the year of her death. During the whole of this time Clare was ill and confined to her bed, as we have seen. But there is no mention of this in these letters. There is, in fact, nothing directly about Clare at all. They contain exhortations and encouragement to the Princess of Bohemia to persevere in her desire to share the life of the Poor Crucified Christ, and to be sure in her heart that it is preferable and more rewarding than marriage to an Emperor. And yet they say everything about Clare, the woman, and her own relationship with the Lord.

## Woman of intelligence

In the Middle Ages the two avenues open for women were marriage or the cloister, and for neither was education, in the academic sense, a prerequisite. We do not know how much education Clare received, but she could obviously read and write, and knew Latin well. However it may have been, what is very obvious from the way her letters are written – and not just from their content – is the quality of her intelligence. They are 'composed'; they have 'shape'; her paragraphs and sentences are balanced. Parts of the letters are poetry; everywhere the language is rich and evocative.

Her genuineness strikes you as she expresses her deepest feelings without moving into sentimentality. There is a calm movement in her style, as her sentences flow towards points of importance. There is a skilful interweaving of scripture and liturgy into her own thoughts. All this shows the strength of her conviction and the measure of her mind. She is writing from her own experience and from a desire to support and uphold a younger woman on her faith-journey. Her intelligence and literary skills are but tools for this purpose. As she is unaware of them, there is not the slightest hint of vanity.

## Her 'way' with Agnes

All four letters have really one subject: how to love Jesus totally. That word 'totally' is most characteristic of her in every aspect of her life. Nothing is undertaken in half measures, and so she shares with Agnes how she came:

to love him totally
who gave himself totally for her love.

When the correspondence began Clare had been living the life for twenty-two years, and she was about 40 years old. Agnes was about 27. She was the daughter of the King of Bohemia. This does not embarrass Clare, nor does she attempt to 'teach' Agnes from her position of greater experience. First, she shows her all the respect due to her rank, and then proceeds very tenderly to affirm the great step Agnes had taken by leaving her royalty and riches behind to follow Christ as Clare was doing. She encourages Agnes to keep going:

What you do may you always do and never abandon.

Second Letter, 11

This is written with such certainty that not only must it have supported Agnes, but it indicates the way Clare habitually acted herself. It shows her to be a woman of great resolve, who would not deviate from what she held to be not only right, but perfect. She pursued perfection, not with rigidity or strain, but gently, with a quietness and lightness of step. In the second letter she wrote, we see this spirit of peaceful calm; her 'way' with Agnes was to take for granted that she would:

Go forward, securely, joyfully and swiftly,
along the path to which the Spirit of the Lord
has called her.

In other words, she shared the strength her faith gave

her with the younger woman so that she too could achieve what she had set out to do – that is *to love him totally.*

This was how she created a strong bond between herself and Agnes. They became 'equals' in their common vision of life. This way of sharing a vision created 'community', so it is no wonder that in the fourth and last letter Clare reveals the great love that has gown up between them over the nineteen or so years, with all the warmth of her heart:

> What more can I say?
> Let the tongue of flesh be silent when I seek to express
> my love for you.
>
> Letter, 4:35

As she invites Agnes to join her in contemplation of Jesus on the Cross, she points to the communion to which their love for him and each other has brought them:

> Let US answer him with one voice
> and one spirit.
>
> Letter, 4:26

You cannot help thinking that if this was the way she related to one she had never seen, how great must have been the bonds she formed with her community whom she saw every day, through these gentle ways of expectation, sharing, affirmation and love.

## Woman of integrity

Perhaps the reason she could identify so compassionately with another was that Clare was a very rounded, thoroughly balanced medieval woman. She wrote much to Agnes of her beloved Jesus. What she cherished in him were qualities that most women look for in a husband. However, Jesus' power is stronger, his generosity greater, his appearance, even, more beautiful; his love, tenderness and respect better than any ordinary husband. Her language is often sensual, drawn both from the riches of this world and of the scriptures. She speaks of Christ's embrace, of him placing precious stones on her breast and pearls in her ears; of sparkling gems and a golden crown. She is a woman of such integrity that she can allow her imagination to be fired by beautiful things and yet be in such peaceful control of her feelings that she in no way averts her gaze from God. In fact, in the first letter these are expressions of Christ's love and his gifts to Agnes.

In the Fourth Letter, written some nineteen years later, Clare shares with Agnes the deepest feelings of her heart in similar language. Christ is so totally her Beloved that he satisfied her in ways that her noble upbringing had formed her to value and which she hadn't forgotten. There is her sense of beauty, the chivalric qualities of graciousness and gentleness; her senses of sight and smell; her memory and her imagination. You can see this is what she writes when speaking of how she relates to Jesus in Holy Communion:

Indeed, she is happy who has the opportunity to
take part in this Sacred Banquet
so that she may cling to him with all her heart.
His beauty is constantly admired by all the ranks
of the blessed in heaven.

Ultimately only the passionate language of the Song of Songs can come near to expressing the true desires of her heart, with such pure joy. Looking forward to her death, she addresses Jesus thus:

> ... and your right hand will embrace me happily
> and you will kiss me
> with the happiest kiss of your mouth.
>
> Letter, 4:32

If you check this reference in Song of Songs 1:2 and 2:6 you will not find the words 'happily' and 'happiest'. Clare added them! The whole thought of being embraced by Jesus in heaven filled her with great human joy!

## Relationships with Jesus lead to mission

It is not surprising, then, that Clare is fully aware of women's role in the Church. Once given to the Lord in poverty and humility, not only do women become *co-workers of God himself*, but also they become his Beloved, his Mother and his Sister. Such roles require the toughness and maturity of a love that does not seek immediate gratification and has the same strength and perseverance that Jesus showed in his Passion. Clare had become so identified with him that by gazing upon him, considering him and contemplating him she had put on that unruffled strength, and so, in the words of the Bull of Canonization, she gave *clear light in the house of the Lord*. There was nothing out of focus about Clare.

In Agnes she had found someone who understood her spiritual language and with whom she could share fully her enthusiasm, ideals, excitement and joy. All of these qualities are only found in someone who is fully alive and full of inner energy. She had discovered another in whom there were no half measures, who realized that God's generosity in showering down his gifts can only be met by TOTAL love, in imitation of the total love of the Incarnation:

> And as you have put aside all those things
> which, in the deceptive and unstable world
> trap their blind lovers,
> love him totally
> who gave himself totally for your love.
>
> Letter, 3:15

She was, indeed, completely freed by her embrace of poverty to love in this way.

## Continually attentive to God

Anyone who saw her as she moved among her Sisters would have been struck by the ring of silence that surrounded her. The 'Life' describes her as being a person who was *sparing in her words, who compressed in few words the desires of her mind.* Behind this exterior silence lay a mind from which every noise had been driven, so that her whole being might be continually attentive to God who dwelt there. The Gospel pivot on which her whole life turned is to be found quoted in the third letter:

> *If anyone loves me he will keep my word, and my Father will love him, and we shall come to him and make our home with him.*
>
> John 14:23

She speaks of this great truth of faith, not in overawed, hushed tones, but in a friendly, everyday way. She paraphrases St John thus: *only the faithful soul can be his home and his comfortable chair.* This homely ordinariness gives us the confidence that it would have been good to live with Clare. This is further confirmed in the Process of Canonization, where several of the witnesses commented that *the holiness and righteousness of the ways of the blessed mother* were such that the Sisters could not fully explain them. Ordinary things are very hard to put into words. Her Sisters must have felt comfortable with her so that they could reach out to meet the challenge of her quiet, but total self-giving to Christ. They would have been affirmed by the genuineness of her love for them and encouraged by her enthusiasm and joy. Love for Christ inevitably leads to love for others.

Clare was, indeed a shining light in the Church of her day, and still is today, but behind that light is a true mystic and a great woman of faith, integrity, love and quiet determination, who, wherever her present-day daughters carry her charism of total commitment to the Gospel into their world, can still inspire people to come closer to God.

## Litany of St Clare

As with St Francis, this Litany of St Clare gives the opportunity to reflect on the Lady Clare's life as a whole and in all its different aspects.

As you ponder on her qualities may you be inspired to come closer to the Lord and grow more like him, as she did.

God – Father of Mercies
God the Son – Radiance of His glory
God – Beloved Spirit
Holy Mary, cherished by St Clare

| | |
|---|---|
| St Clare, daughter of the Most High | Single-hearted Lady |
| Worthy handmaid of Christ | Lady of integrity |
| Beloved of the Holy Spirit | Strong woman |
| Darling of Jesus | Woman full of faith |
| Lover of the Poor Crucified | Woman of hope |
| Dwelling place of the Most High | Contemplative woman |
| Mirror of Christ | Woman of penance |
| Lover of the Eucharist | New woman |
| Little Plant of St Francis | Compassionate Sister |
| Loyal servant of the Church | Selfless Sister |
| Lover of Creation | Courageous Sister |
| Candle of holiness | Loving Sister |
| Clear light of God's love | Refuge of the troubled |
| Brilliant light in the Church | Carer of the sick |
| Seeker after poverty | Lover of children |
| Spiritual Guide | Joy of your Sisters |
| Lady of silence | Footprint of the Mother of God |
| Obedient Lady | Lady of Peace |

## Prayer

Teach us, Good Lord, to learn how to let go of anything in our lives that hinders your love, so that poor in spirit, we may find our greatest treasure in you. We make this prayer through Christ Our Lord.

# Passionate Lovers of Life

God made man in the image of himself,
in the image of himself he created him,
male and female he created them.
And God saw all he had made
was very good.

*Genesis Ch. 1:27,31a*

## A symbol of the relationship between Francis and Clare

There is a picture hanging in the Basilica of St Francis in Assisi by Noccolò da Foligno. It is the earliest known reproduction of the city of Assisi and was painted against the plague in the fifteenth century. Many of the Assisi saints are on it, interceding for the city. The heads and shoulders of Clare and Francis are there, looking upwards, very close together, but not looking at each other. Their interior gaze is fixed on God as they pray for their birth place. Both are young, and both are full of life. This picture symbolizes for me the relationship between these two remarkable people. They are together in everything that matters, because together they do not take their eyes or the centre of their being off Christ who is the source of all their love and the source of their life.

## Francis and Clare meet

So how did their relationship begin? A few dates are helpful here to see their relative ages: 1206 is when Francis heard the voice from the Crucifix in San Damiano, telling him to go and rebuild the church. He was twenty-four then. As we have seen, he understood this quite literally and began with San Damiano. By 1208 he was working with one or two of his early companions on rebuilding the tiny chapel of St Mary of the Angels, a little more than a mile outside Assisi. Francis was about twenty-five or twenty-six, and Clare would have been between fourteen and fifteen. Lady Bona tells us in the Process of Canonization that at this time Clare gave her some money to take to the workers on that church, so they would have something to eat. So Clare must have heard about the amazing change in Francis' behaviour over the past two years, and have been in some way fascinated by it.

It is also clear from the stories the witnesses tell that at this age, when most of her peers would be preparing for marriage, that she had no intention of getting married, because her heart was already drawn to Christ. We have seen how she gave food to the poor and prayed on a regular basis and practised those medieval acts of mortification, like wearing a rough garment under her beautiful dresses. She was a good medieval Christian, with a strong desire to be with Christ. Francis had also been captivated by Christ. Remember Clare did not know about the San Damiano 'incident' but she sensed something special about Francis.

It was to be another couple of years, however, before they met. Around 1210 Clare heard Francis preach in the Cathedral, so her curiosity was further roused. Francis by this time had heard of Clare's goodness and piety and wanted to meet her. In the versified *Life of Clare*, the poet describes their initial meeting thus:

The virgin… desired to see and hear him with an undaunted heart.

They both came together by desire: the holy man longing none the less for her presence.

It is Lady Bona who continues the story by describing how she accompanied Clare many times to speak to Francis. Clare's parents knew nothing of these clandestine meetings, which certainly did not take place in her home. They alternated places and arranged the most convenient times to meet. They were naturally anxious not to be the cause of gossip and to prevent rumours spreading around. They did not want anyone to prevent their meeting. Of course, Lady Bona was curious to know what they talked about. (She must have discreetly kept at a distance while she chaperoned Clare!)

Clare told her that when Francis spoke he lit a fire within her, so that she wanted nothing less than to turn completely to Jesus Christ. Clare drank in his words and his enthusiasm avidly. These meetings, which took place over a period of eighteen months to two years, are the foundation of a deep sharing of spirit in which Christ was magnet which drew them both to him and to each other. The early accounts of these meetings speak of Francis 'preaching' to Clare about leaving all the attractive things of this world, but it is more likely that he retold her Gospel stories in which he made Jesus come alive for her. He would surely have told her how he had discovered just how much Jesus loved him when he had seen and understood the meaning of the Crucifix in the San Damiano chapel. This is how she caught his fire. This is why she wanted to enter the Way which would lead her to Truth and to Life. Each was led by the Holy Spirit, and drawn together into God's love.

So Clare committed herself totally to the guidance of Francis, and he was equally keen to travel alongside her. At this stage of her spiritual life, she "received whatever he said of the good Jesus with a warm heart", says the author of her Life. As for Francis at this time, in sharing with her what he knew of the Gospel, and how he had learnt what God was asking of him, he must himself have grown as he clarified his vision with a kindred spirit. It's as if he took her by the hand and said "Come on, we're leaving all the things the world holds dear and we're going to Jesus to be with him in his poverty."

## Clare's turn to lead

Now it is Clare who takes the initiative. As we have seen, she refuses all offers of marriage to eligible young men, sells her inheritance, and waits for Palm Sunday. Francis and she must have planned her escape together, but it was Clare who showed the strength of this new fire within her as she left home and family in the middle of the night to join, not primarily Francis, but her true love, Jesus. Francis did not show himself to be very practical on this night. He obviously hadn't thought through what to do with Clare once she had vowed herself to God in his hands. Nevertheless he trudges through the night to the nearest Benedictine monastery and leaves her there. He is not there to support her when she is attacked by her family, but immediately Clare realizes that she is in the wrong place, he arranges for her to go to the ladies of Sant'Angelo di Panza. Nor is he there when her sister, Catherine joins her, and is physically attacked by the uncles. Only when he hears that she too wants to consecrate herself to God does he turn up, cut her hair in a round, and receive her vows. Then he directed them both 'in the way of the Lord'.

## Early guidance

Finally Francis suggested that the two sisters make their home in the chapel of San Damiano, and at the beginning he visited them or left them notes of encouragement. He was their only spiritual support at the beginning of this entirely new way for women to dedicate themselves to God. Clare, and Agnes, her sister, were joined that year, (1212) by Sister Pacifica (Lady Bona's blood sister), and Sister Benvenuta of

Perugia. Francis continually watched over them and Clare says that he admired them for what they had undertaken. She writes that he saw "we had no fear of poverty, hard work, trial, shame or contempt of the world." So to guide them further he wrote for them a Form of Life. It was then that he promised for himself and for his Brothers 'always to have the same loving care and special solicitude for you as for them.' What impressed Clare about this simple Rule was that Francis wanted them to continue what they had already begun: to live as daughters and handmaids of the Most High, most Exalted King, the heavenly Father, to take the Holy Spirit as their Spouse, and from this close relationship with God, to choose to live according to the perfection of the holy Gospel. This was the Way Francis gave Clare. It was one with which she was in total agreement, and in Francis' absence it was she who continually encouraged her sisters to follow it. At this time – still 1212 – Francis and his early Brothers were living at the little chapel of St Mary of the Angels, the Portiuncula, just a couple of miles down the road from San Damiano, so it was easy for Francis to communicate with Clare.

## Disagreements and Interdependence

There came that point when Francis asked Clare to take on the role of Abbess, to be responsible for guiding and leading the Sisters. Why did she resist? She trusted Francis, but may be she didn't trust herself? She may have been thinking of the Lord's teaching about humility, and not want to have a 'little kingdom' of her own. Whatever was in her mind, she eventually gave it up and complied with Francis' wise request, but out of this Clare created the role of an

Abbess who served. She was never, like the Benedictines, the Lady Abbess.

There was that other incident when Francis and Clare seriously disagreed with each other over the matter of Clare's rigid regime of fasting. It took both Francis and the Bishop to stop her acting in those excessive ways and to ensure that she ate something every day. She complied by eating little bread and drinking only water! So the strong-willed Clare, at this time aged twenty-one, gave in, because she had promised obedience to God through Francis that day when she left home. Neither of these differences spoiled their relationship, but it does show that they were both very independent people, with ideas of their own. She must have had further discussions with Francis about fasting, because some twenty years later she wrote to Agnes of Prague about the days on which Francis had said there was to be no fasting. She added this for Agnes herself:

> But our flesh is not bronze, nor is our strength that of stone, rather we are frail and inclined to every bodily weakness! I beg you, therefore, dearly beloved, to refrain wisely and prudently from an indiscreet and impossible austerity in the fasting that you have undertaken.
>
> Third Letter, 38

She had really taken on board the lesson that Francis had given her when she was young! All this gave her the experience of true humility through what Francis suggested to her and from his example. Above all, she trusted him to lead her in the right way and he trusted her to listen to him.

Perhaps the most important matter on which Francis trusted Clare's judgment was the time when he was tempted to dedicate his life to contemplation rather that to preaching. Clare's answer, as we have seen, was that he should continue to preach. She saw this as his role in rebuilding the Church, just as hers was to do the praying, together with her Sisters. From these events it seems clear that there was an easy interchange of roles in their relationship. First one, then the other would take the lead, but always both sought to support and cherish the other, because both wanted nothing more than to do what God had called them to do.

## From Francis' point of view

In the many stories about Francis there is very little mention of Clare once she is established at San Damiano. In his own extant writings there is just one message written to her towards the end of his life. He himself at this time was very ill, and had stayed for a while in a tiny hut outside the monastery at San Damiano, where Clare undoubtedly ministered to him daily. So he knew what a tough life they had at that time. Many of the Sisters were sick, caused, no doubt, by the poor diet and overcrowding. Those who were well were exhausted with looking after them. So he wrote an encouraging piece for them. He called them "little poor ones", and urged them not to "look at the life outside, for that of the Spirit is better." He recognized how wearied were those who cared for the sick, and he asks them to bear it in peace. He ends by saying:

Those who are weighted down by sickness and others who are wearied because of them, all of you: bear it in peace. For you will sell this fatigue at a very high price.

His concern for them when he was so suffering himself from sickness and the wounds of the stigmata must have touched Clare deeply.

As we have seen, Francis led a very busy and active life. When he wasn't preaching and travelling from place to place, he was spending days and weeks praying in one of his many hermitages in the hills and forests of Umbria. But not only did he not have much time to spend with Clare and her Sisters, it seems that of set policy he just did not go! He had put into his final Rule in 1223 that no Friar may enter into a monastery of nuns, except those who had the permission of the Holy See. He feared that scandal might arise. By not visiting San Damiano he thought to give good example to his Brothers in the keeping of this Rule.

There may well also have been a hidden agenda: we have seen how hard that he himself had to work to control his sexual desires – excessively hard! Remember the Snow People? So knowing how much Clare meant to him, he deliberately avoided seeing her. This was very surprising to his Brothers, who thought he was being cruel by denying her the pleasure of his company. They seemed to know better than he exactly what he meant to her! This was his reply:

Don't imagine, dear brothers, that I don't love them fully. For if it were a crime to cherish them in Christ, wouldn't it be even worse to have joined them to Christ? Not calling them would not have been harmful, but not to care for them after calling them would be the height of cruelty. But I am giving you an example, that as I do, so should you also do.

Remembrance of the Desire of a Soul, 205

There is touching story in *The Little Flowers of St Francis* which tells how Clare had this wish not just to see him but to eat with him once more. Even though she asked him for this many times, he always refused. So his Brothers said, "Father, it's not according to charity that you keep denying Clare this wish." He replied, "So you think I should give her what she is asking?" They all gave their consent. Then Francis said, "Since you agree, then so do I. And how much more would Clare be pleased if we are to have this meal at St Mary of the Angels, where she first vowed herself to God. After all, she has been enclosed for a long time!"

The day came, and Clare and a companion walked to St Mary of the Angels. She went into the little chapel and greeted the Virgin Mary at her altar where she had received the veil. When it was time to eat Francis had prepared a table on the ground, as he usually did. Then they sat down together, Clare with her companion, Francis with his, and all the Brothers standing around. The story says nothing about food. Francis just started speaking so wonderfully about God, that all of them became rapt in God. They were so full of the Holy Spirit that the people of Assisi got the impression that St Mary of the Angels was burning down in flames, together with the forest that surrounded it. So they rushed down to put it out.

When they got there they saw Francis, Clare and everyone who was there deep in contemplation, and that the 'fire' they had seen was a sign of the fire of divine love in the souls of these men and women.

Now this may be a myth, because *The Little Flowers of St Francis* where this story is recounted, was written about a hundred years after the death of Francis, but like all myths, there is a real truth behind it. Francis and Clare were bonded together by the Holy Spirit, and that is the source of life for them both. It was always present to them, so physical nearness was a bonus, but not of prime importance, as the next incident shows.

Then there was that day when he was pestered by one of the Brothers to go and preach the word to Clare and her Sisters. Eventually he gave in. The Sisters were all ready and waiting. He prayed silently at first, with his eyes raised to heaven. Then he asked for some ashes. He made a circle of them on the floor and then put some on his head all in silence. Clare and the Sisters waited expectantly as Francis stayed in the circle – still in silence. Suddenly he got up and instead of a sermon, he recited the *Miserere – Have mercy on me O God*. When the psalm was finished, he just left. The story goes on to say that the Sisters were full of contrite tears as a result of experiencing this mime at a deep spiritual level. Useful though this incident may have been, Clare herself must have been disappointed that he did not address one word, even to her. She herself says nothing. Who knows how much she understood the heart of this man, who was so wholly at one with Christ?

The year was 1226. Francis was ill. Clare too was so ill at the time that she thought she would die soon, and would not see him before her death. She wept with disappointment because Francis was her comforter in all things, and her first founder in God's grace. Not knowing that Francis was so near death himself she sent a message to him with one of the Brothers about her sorrow at not being able to see him. Francis knew this was impossible, so to console her he wrote his blessing in a letter and pardoned her if, for any way she felt she had not done what he wished her to do. He told her to stop grieving, and inspired by the Holy Spirit he told the Brother messenger to say to her that before her death both she and her Sisters would see him and would be greatly consoled. No more miming, no more silence! Francis died soon after, and the Brothers carried his body to San Damiano so that Clare and the Sisters could see him. They saw the wounds of the stigmata and though they were overcome with both awe and grief, they were comforted by seeing him, just as he had promised they would be. Francis held Clare in his mind and heart, even in death.

## From Clare's point of view

In actual fact, Clare was almost inconsolable when Francis died. Thomas of Celano, in the second part of his first Life of Francis puts into her mouth a tragic lament. Underneath the words and phrases of this expression of her grief is apparent a very deep sense of loss and helplessness. "Who can I trust now? What am I going to do when you no longer come to visit me, enclosed as I am in this cell? Who will comfort me as I experience such a great poverty?" The strength of her true love for Francis is more than apparent in this experience of extreme poverty in the depth of her spirit.

Clare, however, is made of sterner stuff than to succumb totally to this grief. She is to live another twenty-seven years without him, but strong though she was, she never forgot that she was his 'little plant', the first plant of the Franciscan Order, and that they shared the same genes. She spent those twenty-seven years building on their joint project, and continually remembering the things they had dreamt about together.

This is most apparent when she writes her Rule, which is two-thirds taken from the Rule Francis had had approved in 1223. The wording in many places is identical, but little plant though she was, she developed her own life independently of him. Francis, you may remember, would not allow his Brothers to touch money. Clare had money given to a Sister used either for the Sister, or for the common good. In Chapter VI of the Rule she acknowledges the part Francis played in the formation of the community and how he continually encouraged them never to depart from poverty. It was in being faithful to this Gospel teaching, so important to them both, that she had the courage to oppose the Pope himself when he wanted her to accept money and be absolved from her vow. If you read her *Testament* you will feel the presence of Francis in nearly every paragraph. She keeps recalling two things: how he was the instrument by which God enlightened her heart to dedicate herself to him; and how Francis rejoiced at her wholehearted embrace of poverty and all that it entailed in the way of hard work, deprivation and shame. It is here that she speaks not only of the many words of encouragement he gave them, but also of the 'writings', now, alas, lost. Francis may have died, but his spirit lived on: in her mind, in her heart and in the way she continued to embrace life in all its aspects, passionately.

## The dream

In the Process of Canonization Sister Filippa recalled this about a kind of vision/dream that Clare had told her. I will use her words to describe it:

> It seemed to her (Clare) she brought a bowl of hot water to Saint Francis along with a towel for drying his hands. She was climbing a very high stairway, but was going very quickly, almost as though she were going on level ground. When she reached Saint Francis, the saint bared his breast and said to the Lady Clare: "Come, take, and drink." After she had sucked from it, the saint admonished her to imbibe once again. After she did so what she had tasted was so sweet and delightful she in no way could describe it. After she had imbibed, that nipple or opening of the breast from which the milk comes remained between the lips of blessed Clare. After she took what remained in her mouth in her hands, it seem to her it was gold so clear and bright that everything was seen in it as in a mirror.
>
> Process of Canonization, 3:29

This is a strange dream, which has all sorts of overtones. I think one has to remember that for both Francis and Clare everything created by God was beautiful and precious. They never forgot that Christ came from the Father and took on our human nature completely, and so everything about our humanity was doubly precious to them. That is why they both gave such importance to Christ's birth, his passion and his presence in the Eucharist. With this dream, however, I can do no better than to share with you an interpretation of Marco Bartoli in his book *Clare of Assisi*.

It is most likely that Clare had this vision after the death of Francis. During the winter before he died he had stayed at San Damiano, and Clare had probably brought him hot water to wash in, and she would have hurried to the little hut outside lest the water would have got cold. But in the dream Francis is not on level ground but high up, higher than she, which would seem to indicate how she was still depending on him to make progress in her Christian journey. Bartoli reminds the reader that the language of visions or dreams knows no distinction between masculine and feminine. The point is not a physical one, but expresses a meaning in Clare's subconscious. The primitive experience of feeding from the breast is one almost all people have, so Clare is reliving the intense rapport and affection she had for Francis. Francis' invitation to suck a second time simply reinforces this bond of dependence on Francis. The nipple has remained between her lips, as if, like a baby biting the mother as a sign that he/she wants mother to belong wholly to him/her, so Clare here is expressing her longing to make him hers, to become one with him. When she looks at the nipple it is pure gold, a treasure that is her love and friendship with Francis, and much more precious than any worldly wealth she had renounced. It seems to her like a mirror, in which she saw herself as she really was.

There can be no doubt that this vision, the only place where Clare speaks of her relationship with Francis, is an expression of an intense love that was mutual. It was not physical in the way we understand a relationship today, but was founded on their mutual fascination with Christ, and their desire to be like him. Francis had caught it first, and was delighted to be able to draw Clare to Christ as well. They both knew that human love is not a rival to love for God, but draws its strength from God himself. It was this love that continued to inspire Clare to carry on the work Francis had begun by maintaining in her way of life, and that of the Sisters and Convents founded from San Damiano, the primitive ideal of poverty that Francis had striven so hard to maintain among his own Brothers.

## In Conclusion

Apart from the initial meeting between Francis and Clare which is well documented, there are few other places in the Sources which speak of them together. From putting things together in a non-chronological way and deducing largely from what Clare wrote and from the Process of Canonization, it is clear that theirs was a relationship built on mutual respect and affection which lasted all their lives. That Clare relied almost entirely on Francis is evident from some of the words she used to express her affection: she thinks of him as her brother, often calls him 'our Father Francis'. She was not just planted by him, but was his 'little plant'. He had filled her with warmth and the fire of the Holy Spirit as he formed her during those initial meetings. Francis always treated her with tenderness, even when he made demands on her. Such challenges made her strong. When he saw this strength in the way Clare and the others took to this life of poverty, he 'resolved and promised always to have loving solicitude' for her.

That these are not superficial emotions but external signs of a very deep mutual love that was at one and the same time rooted in Christ and expressed through their humanity is most evident in their brief interchanges of messages when they were both so ill at the end of Francis' life. The most powerful sign of Clare's love for Francis lies in the intense expression of her grief at his death and the courageous way in which she remained faithful to the end to all that they had shared together.

# Living Contemplation with Francis and Clare

The Spirit of the Lord will rest upon all those men and women who have persevered in these things and it will make a home and dwelling place in them.

*St Francis, Letter to the Faithful*

## Living Contemplation

I suppose that many people are afraid of the word 'contemplation'. They think of it as something special, reserved for very special people. But it is a way of praying and living that brings people into a really close union with God, so that all their days and ways are filled with his love, and are therefore happy.

We have seen how Francis was at one time in a dilemma: should he spend his life in prayer and contemplation, or should he go around spreading the Good News by preaching? In the end he continued his mission to preach, but he never let go of the importance of contemplation. That is why for his Brothers he wrote a short Rule for Hermitages, in which he planned for four or five Brothers to go into a place for prayer, and two of them would be 'Martha', serving and caring for the others who would spend their time in silence and prayer. Then the roles would be reversed, so that they all could devote time to God.

For both Francis and Clare the essential ingredient for this kind of prayer is silence. Francis himself used to go away into the country alone, where the silence was only broken by the birds or the wind in the trees. Clare's Rule speaks of spending the whole day in silence, except when it was necessary, and then to speak in a low tone. Why is this? Surely it is good to communicate with others? Yes, but it is more important to create a space and place where you can 'listen' to God, invite him into your very person, give him the attention that enables him to touch you. In fact in her Rule Clare gives no specific instruction about meditation or private prayer, because in the silence that is created in the house, the Sisters are constantly open to God, no matter what they are doing. Today most people are so used to the noise of a radio or music on an ipod, or the traffic, or loud conversation that they find silence somewhat threatening. But we have it from the Lord himself, when he puts into the mouth of the prophet Zephaniah: "Be silent before the Lord God! The day of the Lord is at hand!" (Zeph 1:7). And the day when God wants to make himself known to us is everyday!

## Foundations of a Gospel Life of Prayer

When St Clare wrote her letters to St Agnes of Prague her aim was to guide the young Princess into a way of life that was totally given to God. In other words, her correspondence sets out to show her how to live contemplatively, not just when she was at prayer, but throughout all of her day. As Francis had shown her, Clare directed Agnes to faith in the centrality of the Gospel message in its entirety. For Clare it was not just a question of obeying the teaching of Jesus, so much as living like he did, in constant touch with his Father, and by being absolutely true to himself as he experienced human life. Both Francis and Clare called this: following in the footprints of the Poor Crucified.

The first prerequisite for living contemplatively is to desire it above anything else. So Clare confirms Agnes in her choice of dedicating herself completely to God. For sure, both Clare and Agnes chose to dedicate the whole of their lives to God, but what Clare writes in her first letter can also apply to all who are willingly Christians and who want to know what God wants of them:

> You have *chosen* with all your soul and all the *desire* of your heart, most holy poverty and physical hardship, taking as your Bridegroom one of a more noble kind: the Lord Jesus Christ.
>
> First Letter, 6-7

She says directly that when Christ is at the heart of someone's life, then everything else (hardships, etc) falls into place.

It is pretty obvious today that the great attractions for most people are money, with the power that it brings, and sex. Clare deals with both these things head-on: embrace poverty and so become free to let Christ and his values be loved in and through all your relationships. She gives Agnes an image of Jesus that is amazingly tactile. She writes about 'touching him,' 'accepting him'. Today we would probably express this experience as 'getting in touch with him', but whichever way it is described, it is nonetheless real on the level of the spirit. She puts it like this:

> He will make you more pure
> when you touch Him
> You are a virgin when you accept him.
>
> 1:8

She is talking about that integrity, that wholeness of being that comes about when she takes Christ into her heart. Such nearness to Jesus has a purifying effect. When we approach him it is his love that reveals just how we are not being true to ourselves. We have not recognized the bolt holes we escape into in order not to face the dark side of our being. In other words, we are not integrated. Clare explains that the Lord leads us into truer ways of being with great compassion, to purify us, to make us whole, to lead us to be the person he has in mind. For in this love-relationship it is Jesus who takes the initiative to draw us and to love us. Clare puts it like this:

> His power is stronger,
> His generosity greater;
> He is more beautiful to look at;
> He loves more tenderly
> He is more gracious in courtesy.
> You are now tightly held in His embrace.
>
> Letter, 1:9-10

This is the beginning of the life of contemplation according to St Clare. She had felt the truth of the Gospel words: *'You did not choose me, no, I chose you.'* (John 15:14) To respond to this amazing fact just one thing is required: to desire to respond to Jesus' choice. Clare said to Agnes in the very first letter: "You have chosen with … all the desire of your heart … the Lord Jesus Christ." Desire and longing for the Lord is the key that opens up all Clare's spirituality, not just for nuns; it is true for everyone.

Francis expresses this in another way. He sees that it is God who takes the initiative when he writes to the Faithful:

He wishes all of us to be saved through him (Jesus) and receive him with our heart pure and our body chaste. But, even though his yoke is easy and his burden light, there are few who wish to receive him and be saved though him.

In his letter to all the Brothers he prays for "the grace to do for you alone what we know you want us to do and always to desire what pleases you." This is the way to become 'enlightened' and 'inflamed by the fire of the Holy Spirit' so that we can, in fact, be more faithful followers of Jesus Christ. So both Francis and Clare show us that God can do nothing for us without our co-operation and longing for him to be for us a Father, Friend and Inspiration.

## To Christ in prayer

To enable the relationship with Christ that we desire to deepen and grow Clare has some very definite pointers. First, she urges us to be thankful and joyful for the friendship and love Jesus is offering. Our continuing desire for him keeps him close to us. Then she instructs us how to communicate with him, how to pray:

Place your mind in the Mirror of Eternity,
Place your soul in the Radiance of Glory,
Place your heart in the Image of His Divine Being,
and transform yourself completely,
through contemplation,
into the image of God Himself.

3:12-13

In prayer we *place* in Jesus our mind, with all its thoughts and interests; our soul with its aspirations and failures; our heart and everything we desire and love. When you place something you put it down carefully and leave it there. With her three-fold 'place', Clare emphasizes the need to leave our whole being in Christ. Christ is the 'Mirror of Eternity' in which we see what we could not otherwise see: the Father's love for us, going on forever. By looking in that Mirror, which is, in fact, Christ, we also see ourselves, taken up into that love. We look in faith, where the reflection is often 'dim'. We stay there, because by so doing we become drawn into what we so desire: God in his radiant glory, in the very fullness of his Being. Then she says:

> Do this so that you may feel what His friends feel
> in tasting the hidden sweetness which,
> from the beginning,
> God Himself has kept for those who love Him.
>
> Letter, 3:14

The response to this graciousness and courtesy of God can only be to love in return. Not surprisingly then, Clare holds out to us her invitation to

> "Love him totally, who gave himself totally for your love."            Letter, 3:15

To 'love' him totally involves a life of service and loving relationship with others. More than that, though, it is by RECEIVING his love that we become free enough to BE, totally, FOR Christ. The word 'totally' carries with it the need for a commitment to want to live with Christ always, not just when we feel like it or when we have time to spare. In this she is repeating what Francis must have said to her often, and which he wrote to all his Brothers:

> Hold back nothing of yourselves for yourselves,
>     that he who gives himself totally to you
>         may receive you totally.
>
> Letter to the Entire Order

## God's response to our willingness to turn to him

Earlier I mentioned faith. Clare realizes that there is something inestimably precious for the one who lives in the fidelity of this kind of prayer. She says:

> Is it not obvious that by the gift of God,
> the soul of the faithful person is the most worthy
>             of all creatures
>     and is of greater value than even heaven?
> For neither heaven nor the rest of creation
>         can contain the Creator;
> only the faithful soul can be His dwelling place
>             and His home,
> and this comes about only through love, which the
>         wicked do not have.
>
> Letter, 3:22

She then goes on to plunge us right into the heart of the Gospel: The Truth says:

> *If anyone loves me he will keep my word, and my Father will love him, and we shall come to him and make our home with him.*    John 14:23

The gift of his love, which but intensifies our desire to see him face to face, is the Divine Indwelling: God come 'home' to us. It is a gift that we all receive at our baptism, but often come late to realize the treasure that we carry with us all the time. To this closeness and intimacy she guided Agnes, and, as we are so fortunate, ourselves too. Because God has chosen to live within us before ever we choose to live in him, we can be confident that we are loved. We can be comfortable and relaxed about our relationship with God, simply because he has taken the initiative. We do not have to strain to achieve closeness. He gives it to us when we respond to his invitation. Both Clare and Francis discovered and cherished this central message of the Gospel and it permeates everything they said and did.

Francis, however, lays down certain obvious conditions for God to be able to take up his dwelling in our hearts. He says we must give signs that we want to turn away from sin and selfishness to God, by being open to others in love, to be themselves. If we pass judgment on others, he says, we need to do it with compassion; we need to be in control of our love of material things and food and drink, and not let them be in control of us. We need to pray and go to the sacrament of reconciliation and receive Holy Communion. In this way we will be able to imitate Jesus and love our enemies and hate all evil that comes from the heart. Then he says the most amazing thing:

> And the Spirit of the Lord will rest upon all those men and women who have done and persevered in these things and it will make a home and dwelling place in them. And they will be the children of the heavenly Father, whose works they do. And they are spouses, brothers and mothers of our Lord Jesus Christ.
>
> Second Letter to the Faithful

Listen now to how well Clare absorbed this great truth about the closeness of the relationship between the believer and God:

> You have sought the treasures of heaven rather than those of earth… and you are virtually worthy to be called a sister, spouse and mother of the Son of the Most High Father.
>
> First Letter, 23, 24

She got this idea from Francis who explains quite clearly the ways in which we can grow through these ways of seeing ourselves so close to God. He says that we are 'spouses' when we are open to the action of the Holy Spirit; we are 'brothers/sisters' when we, like Jesus, our Brother, do God's will; we are 'mothers' when we carry him in our heart and bring him to 'birth' by our good actions. So all this is not "pie-in-the-sky", but firmly rooted in our every day lives by our every day selves.

## Growth in prayer

Clare has yet another image to help us maintain our contemplative life with Christ. In her Fourth Letter to Agnes she again refers to Christ as a Mirror. She writes:

> Every day look into that Mirror, O Queen,
> Beloved of Jesus Christ.
> Again and again study your face in His
> so that you put on, as you would different kinds of
> clothes, both interiorly and exteriorly,
> all the virtues…
>
> Fourth Letter, 15-17

In this Christ-Mirror Clare is suggesting that in Christ we continue to see things about ourselves we never saw before. Because of his compassion he supports us as we come face to face with behaviours and attitudes that we would hide, even from him. Little by little we realize that he has loved us all along, with all our defects and this encourages us to make every effort to act and react as he would have us do. We have the courage to put on new ways of thinking and acting, as we would put on new clothes.

However, it has been my experience that there is something even more wonderful in this studying of my face in his. To be still, quite silent in my head, and to just look, to gaze into those eyes is where I 'touch' him. I look at him who is looking at me. So now I invite you to do the same. Look at him, looking at you. You are held there by his love. You know yourself to be loved, to be valued, and that it is all his gift. Here the healing of your life takes place. Here you will be aware of growing into the person you have been created to be. But there is a step further still. There are moments when I look into those eyes, and as it were, am drawn through them, into the depths, it seems, of the intimate life of the Trinity. It cannot be described. All I can say is that it leads to stillness and silent worship and praise. I need to emphasize that these are only moments, but more and more they colour the nitty-gritty of everyday life, and hopefully bring the touch of Christ to others in a hidden sort of way.

## Francis on prayer

Francis does not give such specific guidelines on prayer. He invites us to love God and adore him with purity of intention, and he quotes what Jesus said:

> *True adorers, adore the Father in Spirit and Truth…*
> And day and night let us direct praises and prayers
> to him, saying *Our Father, who art in heaven…*
> for we should pray always and not become
> weary.                                   Second Letter to the Faithful

We see how he himself prayed in the prayers that appear within his writings. The centre of his thought is the immense goodness of God which he never tires of repeating and, as it were, soaking himself in it. Listen to this and try to pray yourself slowly into it:

> All powerful, most holy, most high, supreme God:
> all good, supreme good, totally good,
> You who alone are good,
> May we give you all praise, all glory,
> all thanks, all honour
> all blessing and all good.
> So be it. So be it. Amen.
> Prayer at the end of the Praises
> to be said at all Hours

This way of Francis gives a similar experience to Clare when she talks about gazing on Christ. In both instances you can see yourself in a truer light, warts and all. Positively, praying in either way soaks you in the wonder and goodness of God that draws you more intimately to him. Francis' way also takes prayer into everyday life, where we meet so many beautiful things, especially in nature and beautiful people in amongst the weeds! All are kind of footprints of the goodness of God, and move us to think of him and thank and praise him. It all brings joy into our hearts.

## This prayer brings joy

In his Letter to the Galatians St Paul names joy as one of the gifts of the Holy Spirit. In his list of gifts, joy comes second, after love (Galatians 5:22). It is not surprising, then, to find that Clare, who understood so well how to come into the embrace of Christ's love, is full of joy. She is joyful because she, her Sisters, and Agnes have been redeemed in Christ.

She is joyful because of Agnes' progress, so she writes:

> I can be really joyful – and no one can take that joy from me – because I now have what I have always desired on earth, for I can see that you, upheld by a sure sign of Wisdom from the mouth of God Himself, have overthrown, in a marvellous way, the subtleties of the devil and the vanity that infatuates our hearts.                Third Letter, 5-7

The cause of Clare's joy on this occasion appears to be that Agnes has told her about some victories over herself and her natural vanity. Just when we are doing well, and our prayer is going well, and nothing seems untoward in our lives, we suddenly find that we are putting ourselves in the list of saints! It is so easy to attribute to our own efforts our newly acquired goodness, when we need to be thinking that without grace we could do nothing. Our free will so easily slips into bad ways, and this is what Clare calls 'the subtleties of the devil.' But instead of becoming sad because of failing in some way or another, we can joyfully turn to Jesus to heal us and bring us back. This is the 'sure sign of Wisdom' she refers to.

She rejoices because she sees that Agnes, through her desire for union with God, is now a 'co-worker of God Himself, and one who upholds the over-burdened members of His most wonderful Body'. She encourages Agnes not to give in to depression or sadness when she feels herself rejected by anyone, but to be very joyful in the Lord. If you remember Francis' story about Perfect Joy, he rejoiced when life brought him suffering, rejection and pain, because then he felt closest to Jesus suffering in love for us on the cross. A peaceful joy is certainly one of the rewards of the contemplative prayer of gazing and marvelling.

## The joy of Holy Communion

It is not surprising to discover that Clare found that greatest happiness and joy came from Jesus at that high moment of prayer: Holy Communion. She writes in her last letter, not very long before she died:

> She is happy who has the opportunity
> to take part in this Sacred Banquet
> so that she may cling to Him with all her heart.
> Letter, 4:9

She continues to say to us today that it is here that we can marvel at his attractiveness. Beauty is important to Clare and for her, Jesus has a radiant beauty. All heaven shines with it. She sees it manifested in ways that deeply touches us, as he reaches out to us in love. Just to 'look' at him enables us to become new people.

171

When we experience all that he gives us we are fulfilled as we become more and more human, like he is. So Clare is inviting us to reach out to Jesus with all our senses alert so that every part of us may be caught up in responding to his generosity. This may sound an impossible programme, and it cannot all be achieved at once. Indeed, Clare was writing at the end of her life, and she was just a whisper away from seeing Jesus glorious in heaven. But she had spent a life-time doing what she advised Agnes to do – just looking at him with all the intensity of her being.

There is indeed a great sense that Clare is putting her own experience into words, and so telling us that this is on offer to everyone who approaches Christ with faith and love and attentiveness, especially when receiving Holy Communion, and then leaves the rest to him.

Francis, writing small teachings and advice for his Brothers wants them to receive Holy Communion with great faith and tenderness of heart. He makes the presence of Jesus in the Bread and Wine so real when he writes:

> Behold, each day he humbles himself as when he came *from a royal throne* into the Virgin's womb; each day he comes down *from the bosom of the Father* upon the altar in the hands of a priest.
>
> Admonition, 1

He calls on his Brothers to receive Christ with great humility and respect, and to remember that they have eternal life now, when they eat his Body and drink his Blood.

His words are not as intimate as are Clare's, but they have the strength of faith and the scriptures which is always good.

Prayer leads to a desire to follow the footprints of Jesus.

## Loving Service

A life of contemplation is not confined to times of prayer. It spills out into everyday living, if it is at all genuine. Such a life will be founded on the two commandments of Jesus: to love God totally and to love your neighbour as totally as you love yourself. In her letters to Agnes, Clare always refers to herself a "useless servant" of her Sisters. This was no mere platitude. When she was young, even though she was Abbess, she was a foot-washing person, like Jesus. When she was older and became sick, she did become useless and she had to get used to the Sisters doing things for her. Jesus also became 'useless' when he was nailed to the cross. For her every aspect of life was lived out of the Gospel. Francis was the same. He used to live the sayings of the Gospel quite literally, as on the day he threw away his sandals and only wore one tunic at the beginning of his conversion. He was most Gospel orientated in his acceptance of suffering, especially when his ideal was rejected by his Brothers, as his ambition was to follow the footprints of Christ right to the Cross. His 'reward' was to be marked with the wounds of the Crucified. None of these things, however, would have been possible for Clare or Francis had they let the eyes of their attention stray from Jesus and the love he had for them.

## Poverty

The Gospel message which first captured Francis was that invitation of Jesus to the rich young man:

*If you wish to be perfect, go and sell what you own and give the money to the poor and you will have treasure in heaven; then come, follow me.*

Matthew 19:21

Francis did this immediately, and undoubtedly the same Gospel message was the springboard of Clare's spiritual journey. Her community was first called the Poor Sisters, and Clare went to great lengths to ensure that their life-style was truly poor. Not for her were vast acres of land owned by the Benedictines; rich ladies bringing with them large dowries were not among her Sisters. She wanted her community to own nothing, to have no guaranteed income, but to trust for their very lives on the Father's love, who feeds the ravens and clothes the flowers of the field (see Luke 12:22-31). She called this risk the PRIVILEGE OF POVERTY, and she had to hold out for this principle against two popes, who did not like such radical Gospel living. But her quiet determination to be faithful to the Gospel won the day.

Today we might question the wisdom of this but Clare saw poverty as a letting go of what the 'deceptive and unstable world' holds dear: money and all that it can buy to shore up our sense of security; power, whereby we seek to be our own god, the only one in control of events; we negotiate for position, to draw the attention of others to ourselves. Clare says that if we set our hearts on such things then we lose all the benefits of love. We won't have time or mental space

174

to pay attention to God or to other people. She talks about going into God's kingdom through the straight path and the narrow gate. It's pretty obvious you can't get through a narrow gate if both hands are weighed down with carrier bags stuffed with goodies! I remember once going out of the house to visit my sick mother, and I was laden with eggs and flowers. One of the Sisters said to me: "Put everything down so I can hug you!" Ever since, it has struck me how things can get in the way of both giving and receiving love.

Poverty was how she sought to follow the footprints of Christ exactly. She could accept his invitation to sell all that she had because Jesus had come to mean everything to her. For both her and Francis he was more important than possessions or money or houses or land. They felt that the less they had the more room there was for him and his interests. Above all, this was Christ's way. They saw him in the poor stable where nothing of his greatness and majesty was visible. Clare writes, as she looks into the Mirror of Christ's life:

> Pay attention, I say
> on first looking into this Mirror,
> and see the poverty of Him
> who was laid in a manger
> and wrapped in swaddling clothes.
> What amazing humility! What tremendous poverty!
> The King of Angels, the Lord of Heaven and earth
> is laid in a manger!
>
> Fourth Letter, 19-21

Then she looks further into this Mirror, and sees the same humility and poverty expressed in the endless work and hardships of his working life.

> The fox has its lair, and the birds of the air nests, but the Son of Man - that is to say Christ - had nowhere to lay His head, but bowing His head He gave up His very life.
>
> First Letter, 18

In the end the Mirror becomes Jesus on the cross, and her spirit is filled with sadness. Yet here, in the life and Passion of Jesus, is where she finds the love that she had spoken of so frequently in her letters. She now invites Agnes and us to "let yourself be burned up with the intensity of this love again and again." Her contemplative life was built on the Gospel, and on her relationship with the Jesus she found in the Gospel, and that is why her two key virtues are humility and poverty. Without these there can be no love for anyone – not even oneself!

Strangely enough Francis *says* little about poverty, but his life was lived in great poverty. Nothing got in between him and God's love for him, and he did encourage Clare never to let go of the poverty she had promised the Lord. His Italian name was Poverello, the little poor one. Both of them certainly shared what little they had with others who had less, especially clothes!

## Poverty brings freedom and fulfilment

All through Clare's writings she is saying that poverty is the soil in which a deep relationship with Christ will flourish. In this twenty-first century more than half the world lives in poverty and the rich half is constantly encouraged to alleviate it. We see poverty and destitution as bad things. We remember that Jesus said that the poor would be with us always. So what is Clare's idea of poverty? She herself, and her Sisters too, lived entirely on the good will of the people of Assisi who brought or gave them the necessities of life. They had no set income at all, their clothes and their accommodation and their food were frugal. They CHOSE this way of life, whereas there were then and certainly are now, millions of poor who do not choose poverty. The Sisters chose it, and still do today, because of their desire for God and trust in his love.

The main desire of people today is to possess more and more. It is constantly fed by adverts and attractive shopping malls, so that we become imprisoned by whatever money can buy. We are somehow not free to stop 'shopping' - either in reality or in our imagination. 'Things' are so tangible and attractive that the life of faith can become elusive and/or irrelevant. 'Things' boost our security, our relevance and importance in society, and we rely on them almost exclusively.

It depends, therefore, what we want most, what we feel to be most valuable. If we are content to be compulsive 'shoppers', then we will be forever shut in by desires that are never satisfied. If, however, we realize that this way of thinking precludes a deep relationship with both God and others, then we are being invited to set our longings towards another goal.

How then did the rich girl, Clare, and the extremely rich Princess Agnes, cope? They saw in the love that Jesus showed them something infinitely attractive. He inspired them with passionate love and they made for him an empty room in their hearts. Clare wrote to Agnes:

> For a camel will be able to go through the eye of a needle before a rich man can climb into the kingdom of heaven. It is because of this that you have thrown away all your rich clothes, your worldly things, lest the wrestler utterly overpower you, and so that you might go into God's kingdom 'through the straight path and the narrow gate.'
>
> First Letter, 28

Once more, happiness predominates; Clare has found that poverty creates it, because it gives eternal wealth - freedom - to those who love and welcome it freely. The 'eternal' has already begun! We don't have to wait till we die to begin it! Such poverty, chosen with faith and joy, can bring us fulfilment. Certainly most people are not in a position to 'sell all'. It is a question of becoming, in faith, secure enough in God's care for us that we are able to share what we have with others, knowing that we are in the embrace of our loving Father.

Clare is a tremendous optimist. She is always looking for the better rather than the merely good thing, and when she finds it, she is overjoyed. The best thing for her is always poverty, so that she could be open to a greater awareness of God, of his presence in her life, and of his love for her. God was always truly God in her world. She never mentions the word 'freedom', but in twenty-first century understanding, this is what her kind of poverty leads to. She is not speaking about destitution, though she and her Sisters did lead a life without frills. She exhilarates in the way *chosen* poverty enables you, frees you, to be completely open to God and to love, and so to be happy, because God is the only one who can completely fulfil you. Living with this attitude is to live a life of contemplation. Though Francis does not explain poverty like this, she most likely developed ideas they had talked about in the beginning of their relationship.

**What about sin?**

Francis' big theme in his preaching was to turn away from sin and turn towards God and his love. This is what he called 'conversion' – a turning to something better. It was the first thing he called his new Brothers, and the men and women who joined the Third Order to do. He has great lists of the things they must stop doing, like jealousy, pride, avarice, irreverence, greed and the like. These had to be replaced by the virtues. He writes a lovely poem in praise of the virtues. It begins:

Hail, Queen of Wisdom! May the Lord protect you,
with your sister, holy pure Simplicity!
Lady holy Poverty, may the Lord protect you
with your sister, holy Humility!

Then follows Charity and Obedience, and he goes on to describe how these virtues overcome evil, desire for riches and pride, so that all life comes under the influence of the Spirit and so people become free to choose the good.

Sin is not a fashionable concept today. It might seem that whoever seriously strives to live con-templatively would not become involved with sin. Quite the contrary! Clare knew very well the temptations that could get the better of those who were striving to be completely open to God's love. In her Rule she writes:

I admonish and exhort the sisters in the Lord Jesus Christ to beware of all pride, vain glory, envy, avarice, care and anxiety about this world, detraction and murmuring, dissension and division.                    Rule 10:6 & 7

She must have seen all these sins around her in the community, for they are almost inevitable in a group of women living on top of each other. No one escapes the penalties of original sin!

In another place she stresses one of the most radical and most difficult teachings of the Gospel when she stipulates the absolute need for forgiveness of one by another:

> If it should happen that an occasion of trouble or scandal should arise between sister and sister through a word or gesture, let she who was the cause of the trouble... ask pardon... Let the other sister, mindful of that word of the Lord "if you do not forgive from the heart, neither will your heavenly Father forgive you" generously pardon her sister every wrong she has done her.
>
> Rule 9:6-10

Clare speaks frequently of the way in which the devil can subtly tempt people into pride and vanity. She encourages Agnes to battle with such temptations by cultivating humility, faith and poverty. She has learnt this from Francis. It is when we recognize our weaknesses and present them in all poverty to the Lord, that he is able to give us his mercy.

There is nothing in Francis' Rule quite like this. His emphasis in all that he writes is on loving our enemies and putting up with those who offend us. He is for ever on the watch how to become more like Jesus in his Passion. However, in his Prayer inspired by the Our Father he says this:

> *As we forgive those who trespass against us*:
> And what we do not completely forgive, make us,
> Lord, forgive completely
> that we may truly love our enemies because of you.

In his Earlier Rule of 1221 he tells the Brothers to be 'careful not to slander or engage in disputes'. Instead they are 'to keep silence whenever God gives them the grace'. Most positively he encourages them to 'love one another, as the Lord says… Let them express the love they have for one another by their deeds'. Each in their own way say the same thing: it is best to accept people and the way they behave towards us as they are, and with love.

Finally, in her last of the four letters to Agnes, she describes the success of their journey, saying: "You have been marvellously espoused to *the spotless Lamb who takes away the sins of the world.*" Is she not saying that to be free from sin depends on accepting the love that Jesus is giving us, as a husband gives love to his wife? So, far from ignoring the fact of sin, Clare is fully aware of its presence in everyone's life. Her whole spirituality presents us today with remedies against it, as she invites us to a way of life that follows Christ implicitly.

**And the Darkness?**

From time to time in our spiritual journey we hit times of darkness, when God seems to be 'out'. We do not seem able to get in touch with him at all. All the old ways that were so fruitful in the past don't 'work' any more. There is a crisis of faith, as we wonder if indeed we have imagined the whole thing, and that there is no God after all. We are desolate, and scratch around our conscience to find some sin that is, may be, blocking the way with no success.

Just before she died Clare asked to make her confession. Sister Filippa who was there, said: "She made such a beautiful and good confession that I have never heard anything like it. She made this confession because she doubted that she had not offended in some way the faith promised at her baptism." From this it would seem that Clare had experienced this very darkness, had known what it was to be left alone by God, and wondered if she had sinned against faith. This is the only hint we have of such a happening, but we know that whatever were her trials, she never stopped being with Jesus on the Cross, for he also had experienced being abandoned by God. In her last moments she received much consolation from God, as she was drawn deeper into relationship with the mystery of the Trinity. To endure such dark times with hope and faith springs from living contemplatively.

## The importance of the Word of God

Both Francis' Rule and Clare's Form of Life begin with an avowal 'to observe the Holy Gospel of Our Lord Jesus Christ.' Francis writings are shot through with the words of the Bible which he was able to choose at random to make his point. We have already seen how important the Word of God was to him if ever he saw parts of it thrown down. It was the same for Clare. There was no bible at San Damiano. She never says anything about spiritual reading or studying the scriptures, but her own life was shot through with an in-depth knowledge of the Word of God. How did she acquire it? We know they had a Breviary, but that is all. Like Francis what she knew came to her through listening to the scriptures read at Mass and in the Divine Office, and herself reciting daily the psalms, canticles and responses in the Liturgy. In her six writings there are thirty-four references or allusions to St Matthew's Gospel alone, to say nothing of the allusions to seventeen Old Testament books, and nineteen in the New Testament! The letters particularly reflect a sensitive response to the Liturgy of her times. This was clearly her way into the mind and heart of Christ, and she would take it for granted that we would under gird our spiritual life with Lectio Divina and Scripture Reading to build our response to God on the same firm foundation that she did. There is no other way.

## Root yourself in Christ

The contemplative spirituality of both Francis and Clare can be summed up very simply. They would say to us: root yourself in Jesus' love for you and desire him with all your being. Empty out of your system all other desires that have a hold on you, put everything down, so that there is room in your heart for him and for others. Let your desire for him lead you into the prayer of gazing and 'placing' yourself in his love, of adoration, praise and thanksgiving. Try to live your life following the footprints of Jesus. Keep his Passion and Death and Resurrection in mind, and see what this says to you in your circumstances. Confirm all this by a constant habit of browsing in the scriptures and taking an active part in the liturgy. Such a programme will most certainly lead you to joy and to fullness of life.

However, some busy people may murmur that they would never have time for such a programme of prayer, Scripture browsing, Mass, Sacraments, when life is filled with the job, travelling, family, social life, etcetera. Surely such a regime is meant only for contemplative Sisters?

There is a way round this problem of time. Both Francis and Clare say:

> Above all we must desire to have the
> Spirit of the Lord
> and his holy manner of working.

It does not take 'time' to desire this, to ask for the help of the Holy Spirit - perhaps while we are cleaning our teeth! We always manage to do what we want to do! So our problems will disappear as we do what is reasonably possible for us. The Spirit will bring our small efforts to fruition, as he permeates every aspect of our life, not just the 'holy' bits!

So we are brought to a greater fulfilment and 'do well' in the Lord, as Clare would say. We become a sign to others of the love with which the Spirit has filled us. We will be truly living contemplatively.

# Read more about St Francis and St Clare

## St Francis

*Francis of Assisi – Early Documents*. Edited by R.J. Armstrong OFM Cap., J.A. Wayner Heliman, OFM Conv., William J. Short OFM. New City Press London, 1999, Volumes 1 & 2.

*The First Life of St Francis of Assisi*, Thomas of Celano. Trans Christopher Stace. SPCK, 2000.

*The Reluctant Saint*, Donald Spoto. Viking Compass, 2002.

*Francis of Assisi*, Arnaldo Fortini. Crossroads, New York, 1981. (For the avid reader!)

*Brother Francis of Assisi*, Ignacio Larranaga. Mediaspaul, 1989.

*The Life and Times of St Francis*, Portraits of Greatness series, Hamlyn, 1967. (Good pictures.)

*St Francis of Assisi*, G.K. Chesterton. Hodder and Stoughton, 1996.

*Little Flowers of St Francis*, available in various editions, paperback and hardback.

*Francis of Assisi*, Adrian House. Pimlico, 2000.

*Living the Incarnation*, Sister Frances Teresa OSC. DLT, 1993.

*Praying with Francis of Assisi*, Stotenberger and Bohner. St Mary's Press, Winona, Minnesota, 1989.

## St Clare

*St Clare of Assisi, The Lady* – Early Documents. Revised and expanded by Regis J. Armstrong, OFM Cap. New Press London, 2005.

*Clare A Light in the Garden*, Murray Bodo OFM. St Anthony Messenger Press, 1992.

*Praying with St Clare of Assisi*, Miller and Patterson OSF. St Mary's Press, Winona, Minnesota, 1994.

*This Living Mirror,* Reflection of St Clare of Assisi. Sister
    Frances Teresa OSC DLT, 1995.
*In the Footsteps of St Clare,* A Pilgrim's Guide Book,
    Ramona Muller OSF. Franciscan Institute, New York.
*Clare of Assisi,* Mark Bartoli, translated by Sister Frances
    Teresa OSC, DLT, 1993.